Shanta & R

Thank you so much
for your love and
wisdom.

I belong to you

♡

Florencia Clifford

Feeding Orchids to the Slugs
Tales from a Zen Kitchen

Florencia Clifford

 Vala

First published in 2012 by Vala Publishing Co-operative

Copyright © Florencia Clifford

Vala Publishing Co-operative Ltd

8 Gladstone Street, Bristol, BS3 3AY, UK

For further information on Vala publications, see

www.valapublishers.coop or write to info@valapublishers.coop

Illustrations, design and typography by Michaela Meadow

www.michaelameadow.com

Typeset in Freya, designed by Saku Heinänen

Printed and bound by CPI Antony Rowe, Chippenham, UK

The paper used is Munken Premium, which is FSC certified.

No Guru, No Church, No Dependency by John Crook

is reprinted with the kind permission of his family.

Some of the names in the book have been changed.

A CIP catalogue record for this title is available from

the British Library.

ISBN 978-1-908363-03-9

How to use this book

This is a book about the journey of learning to be a Zen cook. It is about cooking, and the stories that arise when you are cooking. It is about the healing that occurs when you can look at your problems face to face and make friends with your ghosts. Although I cook mainly at the Maenllwyd, I also cook for Buddhist retreats in other parts of the country, and I cater for the teacher-training courses in my local Steiner School.

Whilst I have included recipes, my style of cooking is instinctual. It is about connection and experiment. I do not plan menus. I am inspired to create meals by ingredients in season: meals emerge out of the mood of the retreat. Each day is fully creative, and slowly the dormant artist in me, my hidden, wilder self, has emerged through my cooking.

Please use the recipes as a guideline. Although they have been tested, there is always room in a recipe to make it yours. Chop the vegetables in the shape you'd like them to be, think of colours and presentation. Get to know your ingredients: from the moment you source them, to the preparation, to the cooking, to the offering, to the eating.

And before you start, learn to really taste your food, as this will help in your cooking. Try this exercise in meditative eating with a handful of mixed fruit and nuts. Pour the contents into the palm of your hand, and place one of them at a time in your mouth. Close your eyes, feel the shape as your fingers pick it up. Notice the texture in your palate, don't think about anything, feel it as you chew it, notice where the flavours move inside your mouth, how it feels like when you swallow, what it tastes like. Take your time, don't rush it. Are they similar in taste? Pay attention to what happens when the dried fruit begins to hydrate in your mouth. Do you know what you are eating? Where has it originated from? Think of the person who harvested it, packed it, then return to the taste. Once you have practised with fruit and nuts, try it out with a meal.

Florencia Clifford

Foreword

In the early part of the 13th century C.E., a young Japanese Buddhist monk, disenchanted with the stagnation of the teaching in his native land, left on a long and perilous journey to China to find a teacher who could guide him to enlightenment. On his way, he met an old monk, the Chief Cook from A-Yu-Wang Mountain monastery, who through example and simple instruction was to have a profound effect on the young seeker's awakening. The traveller's name was Eihei Dogen, and he was to become the founder of the Soto Zen school of Japan, and one of the most influential teachers in the history of Zen. One of his seminal written works is entitled *Instructions to the Cook* (*Tenzo Kyokun*) and to this day, the cook is considered the most important and respected person in a Zen monastery. Why? In describing one woman's path to becoming such a cook, this lovely, honest, revealing book goes some way to providing an answer.

I first met Flo in the kitchen of a retreat centre on the edge of Dartmoor. I was acting as Guestmaster for a retreat being led by Jisu Sunim, a Korean Zen master, and she, of course, was acting as cook. Although we had both been connected for many years with retreats at the Maenllwyd, a remote retreat centre in the wild hills of mid-Wales, our paths had for some reason never crossed before. I was impressed by how she was able to immediately inhabit this new space, and quietly, efficiently and mindfully organise it for the coming week. A Zen retreat cook's life is not easy. The schedule begins with rising at 5 am, and ends with bedtime at 10 pm. During this time, the cook needs to produce breakfast, lunch and evening meals. Although she has help from assistants drawn from the participants (work periods are an important part of retreat practice), it is the cook's responsibility to ensure that all the food is ready at the appointed time, that there is a sufficient amount (but no excess), and that any participants with specific dietary requirements are catered for. She must organise the preparation, serving and cleaning up of the meals and the cleanliness of the kitchen. She is also expected to participate in as much of the retreat schedule as her workload allows.

This then is the external activity of the Zen cook. But there is far more to her contribution than this. The Master's work is of course to guide and offer teaching, to care for the spiritual life of the retreat. The Guestmaster's job is to oversee the smooth running of the centre, to organise the complexities of a group of people living in close and silent proximity, to manage the temporal aspects of the event. One might say that the cook's role is to bind these worlds together, for of course the temporal and the spiritual are not in fact separate and are seldom more intimate than when we mindfully partake of food. In many ways, the Zen cook could be seen as a manifestation of *Kwan Yin*, the Bodhisattva of Compassion, She Who Hears the Cries of the World. A Zen retreat is no holiday: it is often a time of deep self-encounter, and this may lead to the surfacing and release of much suffering as well as joy. Flo's kitchen becomes a place of refuge, where a cup of tea, a piece of home-made cake, or even just the warm glow of a Rayburn and the wonderful aromas of slowly cooking food can bring a return to peace, balance and gentle determination.

Flo has a knack of knowing what is needed, and of quietly, unobtrusively and appropriately providing it. Her cooking reflects the spirit of mindfulness and compassion that is at the heart of Zen: her dishes are not only deeply nourishing to the body, but renewing to the spirit. They are beautiful to look at, not from ostentation but from a recognition that in presenting food beautifully we are honouring all the beings who have made the presence of this meal possible, and the deep and unbreakable interconnectedness of all existence. Her choice of ingredients and how they are combined are skilfully connected to the current "mood" of the retreat: Flo's menus are responsive, not set. And like all good Zen cooks, Flo recognises that her work in the kitchen reflects her work with her self. Cooking is not a task, or a job, but a practice. This takes real courage for, whilst the practice of the retreatants sitting on their cushions is invisible to others, the cook's practice is revealed to all with every meal she serves.

So please, savour this book as you would a Zen meal: putting aside expectations, classifications and comparisons, taste each morsel, see how it resonates with your own practice, your own experience, your own work. And although there are many delicious recipes tucked inside these pages, the main one is this: in responding to each moment with authenticity, inquiry, compassion and mindfulness, we truly encounter the wonder of our lives.

Ned Reiter (*Guo Ji*), Registered Medical Herbalist
Somerset, July 2012

In memory of my teacher

John Hurrell Crook (*Chuan-deng Jing-di*)

For my parents, Ian and Anita

and my children, Ian and Sofia

Contents

Prologue

Love makes you see a place differently, just as you hold differently an object that belongs to someone you love. If you know one landscape well, you will look at all other landscapes differently. And if you learn to love one place, sometimes you can also learn to love another.

~ Anne Michaels, *Fugitive Pieces*

I was born and grew up in Córdoba, a mountainous region right in the middle of Argentina, splashed with blue hills that stretch west towards the Andes. For the first half of my life, I was embraced by slopes of rock and grasses, pink peppercorn trees, open skies and the Southern Cross.

For the past two decades, living in York, away from my native landscape, it is the mountains I have missed the most. I have recurring dreams in which I open my kitchen window and I see the outline of the cerulean hills undulating on the horizon. Places shape your life and sway you in a lasting way; they imprint you.

Although I grew up in Argentina, I always felt a strong sense of familiarity with Britain. My paternal ancestry is Scottish, but even though we never interacted with the ex-pat community, remnants of my grandparents' heritage and culture tinted our lives in different ways. I clearly remember the feeling of melancholia, of homesickness, that came to me in waves, when I thought of Britain. As a child I longed for the wilderness of Scotland. I proudly showed my friends the family tartan and listened to The Beatles and Highland music on vinyl. We dreamt of riding double-decker buses in London, of hearing Big Ben, of walking around the foggy streets, even though I remember Grandpa saying that London smelled of sprouts.

My sister Magda and I made up Scottish dances in the living room. In the summer, we spent part of our holidays in El Reposo in Ongamira, a remote place in the mountains where Grandpa took us because it reminded him of Scotland. He had never lived in Scotland, it had never been his home, yet he felt nostalgic about it, and so did we. A yearning embedded in the family's way of being flooded our silences.

At school, my sisters and I were considered *Inglesitas* (little English girls) during the Falklands War, and some of our classmates treated us like the enemy. The extended Clifford family gatherings were carried out partially in English: we drank leaf tea in china cups and ate scones with jam, drop scones with savoury toppings, cucumber sandwiches and fruitcake.

Some of our relatives even had a portrait of the Queen in their living room. The fascination with all things British meant that their houses were full of tea caddies, cake tins, thimbles, tea towels and naff souvenirs with pictures of the latest royal wedding. There was a sense of nostalgic pride and celebration. After a visit by my great uncle and aunt to London in 1981, we were showered with Charles and Di engagement souvenirs: a jigsaw puzzle (on which I can vividly remember the bluebird print of Diana's shirt) and two celebratory mugs, which we kept in the kitchen as kitsch ornaments. The presence of the mugs aroused suspicion amongst our neighbours when the war broke out, and one knocked on our door to find out what we intended to do with them. Dad suggested we built a big bonfire in the street, in which we would burn the mugs, publicly displaying our loyalties. He was being ironic, but in truth, we did not support either side. We used to listen to the BBC World Service on our short wave radio, so we could get the other side of the story.

Whenever I look back at my ancestors, I see people leaving their homes in Europe to make a new life, to inhabit the new world. Buenos Aires had opened its doors to the world towards the end of the nineteenth century with a candid and alluring invitation to a sanctuary, to a land that was rich and wild, in need of population. People flocked in ships from all over Europe, from Syria, from Lebanon, from Armenia. Eastern European Jews escaping pogroms; Italian peasants looking for their only chance of owning the land they farmed; Welsh émigrés attempting to maintain their Welsh ways, settling in Patagonia; the French; the Basques. The British invested more money in Argentina at the start of the 20th century than they did in India Argentina is a melting pot where people mingled and settled and worked hard to build a nation, but the collective unconscious was, at the time when I was growing up, soaked up with melancholic cries for home.

My own experience as an émigré led me to identify with my grandmother, Mary. She met my grandfather, Alec, on a train journey from London to Glasgow. Mary was being harassed by a drunk and Alec, who was visiting his father's home town, interfered. They started chatting, realised they were going to the same place, and soon began courting. Alec returned to Argentina and after exchanging letters for a few months, she agreed to marry him. On her own, she made the long voyage by ship to Buenos Aires. They married in the docks, as soon as she landed, as a law had just been passed to prevent single, unaccompanied women from entering the country. At the time many immigrant women were being tricked into prostitution.

Thirteen years and three children later, she managed to return to Scotland, for a visit that lasted two years. My dad was only a small baby. She only ever made two trips home to see her family again. They never managed to visit her. She died when I was six, a frail, gentle lady who hardly spoke when we were around; my memories of her have faded.

I can see myself, holding on to the doorframe of her bedroom in the house next door to ours. I see her, a tiny woman in pristine white bed-clothes, bedridden. Her bedroom had a French, triple-door, rococo armoire with a mirror, which momentarily held both our reflections: a little girl tiptoeing quietly, like an outsider, watching from a distance, attempting to connect to the woman with the long silver hair lying on a bed, staring out of the window. I vividly remember this room, which smelt of medicine and flowers. She died in that room and we were whisked away in the middle of the night to stay with my other grandmother in the country. I think I must have been taken whilst I was asleep, because I remember waking up in a different bedroom and hearing the grown-ups whispering to each other. The words were almost lost in the hush of the early dawn and in the rustle of people coming in and out, but I knew she was gone. We were told properly later that day and we did not attend the funeral. She suffered from heart disease and my dad tells me that the symptoms were made worse by her depression and homesickness: the longing for home got hold of her and took her while she was still relatively young.

We were obsessed with British ingredients. We adored Cadbury's chocolate, Twining's tea, Coleman's mustard powder mixed with water in a little silver and blue glass dish which accompanied our roast beef. On Sunday nights we used to have a few drops of Lea & Perrin's Worcester sauce in our simple broth with handfuls of tiny pasta shapes, to compensate for an undoubtedly enormous lunch in the country at my maternal grandparents' house. We also liked a splash of Lea & Perrin's on crispy fried eggs. There was a time when my parents were hard up and we ate a lot of eggs.

Our interest wasn't confined to British food – we loved the foods of the empire. We sprinkled curry powder on white rice, and my dad would buy exotic spices from a shop in Buenos Aires called *El Gato Negro*. He used to go to Buenos Aires to work a lot when we were kids, and on one of his trips he discovered the shop so he brought back the brochure. It contained long lists of tea blends, a wide selection of coffee beans from around the world, and spices. The brochure was black, red and white with a picture of a black cat, Belle Époque-ish, which spoke more of the Moulin Rouge than of an exotic spice shop. My mum, thinking my dad had been to a cabaret, threw the brochure back at him and stormed off. I still grin when I think of that brochure, and I have visited the shop in Calle Corrientes a few times: a fascinating, turn of the 20th century store, with oak counters and ash shelves, bronze chandeliers and Thonet chairs. The smells are captivating, the spices impregnate the air, and the coffee beans are roasted in the original machine. You can sample the blend of your choice in a perfect espresso. It has now been named a historic heritage site.

Although there is no legacy of recipes that have been passed down from the Scottish side of the family, apart from poached egg on toast, and drop scones which we ate with the Argentinian staple, *dulce de leche*, I think that my curious and adventurous palate came from that innate curiosity for new flavours that most British people have. We were, in a culinary sense, a lot more adventurous than most people we knew. And yet, amongst all the exotic favourites, there were flavours and predilections that I found hard to fathom: my grandfather's love for Bovril on toast, for spam, for tinned corn beef sandwiches. In a country where you could eat fillet steak every day, these British war-time substitutes for "real" meat were unnecessary, yet I imagine he chose them because he relished the connection, they fed his melancholia. Food can do that; it can bring you that warmth of home in one evocative mouthful. So I see him, my Grandpa Alec, my gentle giant, sitting alone in his kitchen, with a cup of tea and a book by his side, eating

4

his English food, thinking of his parents, of his wife, of his dead daughter, Betty, of the Fairlie Moors. The constant longing of the émigré lived in him and in all of us. The loves were lost, yet returned, momentarily, in each bite.

He encouraged me to read and as a child I devoured books; we had an impressive library. I read Penguin Classics and Ladybird children's picture books. *Shopping with Mother* was my first glimpse into British shops, bakeries and iced buns, meat wrapped in waxed paper, sweet shops. Those books were like small windows into British suburban life, traditions, wildlife. Later I began to take books from the big bookshelves: Wilde, the Brontës, Dickens, Sir Arthur Conan Doyle, all books that fed my imagination, connecting me with the culture and landscape of the British Isles.

As I became a teenager, the longing and fascination shifted towards music. It was the mid 1980s. The military dictatorship, or *junta*, had ended and suddenly there was a new wave of music, from both Argentina and abroad. It was freely available although sometimes difficult to get hold of. I travelled to English cities in my head through music, from my bedroom, through a cassette player and the first FM radio stations. I slept with music, woke up with music and found an indie-pirate record store that managed to get rare imports from the UK. They made compilation tapes of my favourite songs or I recorded over my dad's TDKs from shows on pirate radio stations. Perhaps it is true, as a friend of mine says, that despite not being a colony, we too were victims of the empire. The hidden empire imposed a language that wasn't ours, and music that didn't belong to our experience. But I was happily colonised by David Bowie and Peter Gabriel, by The Cure, by Japan, by Joy Division. This was music that meant something to me, that resonated with my inner angst, with my being.

So it is perhaps no surprise that I fell in love with an Englishman, Simon, during a gap year in the US, when I was in my early twenties - especially after I checked his music collection and his cooking skills - and that we both chose Britain as a place to settle down and raise our children, as a place to build our own home.

My first British visit was to the Isle of Wight, to meet my in-laws. I remember the weather. I felt cold, a cold I had never experienced before: damp, trenchant. Not even sitting next to the coal fire in their charming cottage warmed me up. Yet I felt an uncanny familiarity with the place, although the social norms of Simon's family felt alien to me. I suspect that my ancestors had soaked up the spontaneity and warmth of the South American way of life, and had renounced the composed approach of the British to relationships. It was, however, a very special time. My mother-in-law, Lucy, was perhaps the best cook I have ever met, and I relished the dishes she prepared. We feasted on three or four Christmas dinners in just one week's visit. I can still taste her treacle sponge pudding!

We moved to York. It took me a considerable time to settle down, although on the surface I probably seemed to assimilate without much effort. I was eager to lay down some roots, but the internal struggle was intense. There was a complicated social code that I needed to adhere to if I was going to integrate, and it felt, at times, like putting on a straitjacket. Although I felt more at home in England than I did in the US, my Latin essence was suddenly more visible and it was screaming "let me out".

Now, after nearly two decades in the UK, the word home describes different spaces. Home is the house I inhabit with my family, in Yorkshire: the quirky abode I created with my husband and my children; the walls and objects that surround me; the cherry tree in the back garden; my friends; the neighbourhood. But on Sundays and at Christmas and during the winter in particular, I miss Argentina and my family and friends desperately. It is like missing home, from home. There is the home of my everyday life: the sound of Radio 4 when I walk into the kitchen; the morning walks I take with Pirate, my dog; my visits to London, or to the moors. But another home also permeates, as Piazzola plays in my living room, spinning me back to a round of maté tea underneath the china-berry trees in my grandmother's garden. I savour memories of quick espressos in a Buenos Aires pavement cafe, of a natter with my siblings, of the drive from Cordoba to La Granja with the obligatory stop at the bakery in El Pueblito for little squares of flaky pastry and dulce de leche. A picnic by the river, a barbecue with friends, Christmas day spent eating leftovers and swimming outdoors, the social gatherings with the extended family, sitting outside late into the night, a sky so laden with stars it feels it might drop on you.

A few years ago, I still felt as if I lived my life with one foot in Argentina and another in England. When I was here I wanted to be there, and vice versa. Life was difficult for me and for those around me. I knew I needed to settle, somewhere, but I could not find the tools with which to do it. Living with constant yearning left me feeling split; two personas inhabiting different worlds, swapping longings.

An encounter with a farmhouse in Wales, on the mountain where the path ends, and where I could see the lush terrain going upwards from the kitchen window, came as a much-needed catalyst for change. It was here that I began, and where I continue, my journey of Zen practice, cooking and healing.

Chapter One

A Welsh Farmhouse

No guru, no church, no dependency.
Beyond the farmyard the wind in the trees.
The fool by the signless signpost
Stands pointing out the way.

~ John Crook

The Maenllwyd ("Grey Stone" in Welsh) is a retreat house in mid-Wales, set in a beautiful valley. It is an old farmhouse, linked to the main road by a mile of rough track, punctuated by several gates, each of which need to be opened and closed again as you drive up.

The Maenllwyd is a refuge, a house of rough-cut stones shaped to fit. Some parts are hundreds of years old. It is assembled from a mish-mash of local stone and wood, anchored by the stones of the mountain beneath the soil. It is woven into the landscape by ancient tracks and the tumbling stream to the dreamy rolling valleys below, and the heather-clad windswept peaks above.

It is a farm, but it remains a wild and natural place, a place that is air, time, water, and fire. The landscape has been shaped by erosion and weather and farmers and dwellers, by hermits and worshippers, by the rain and the wind. Sheep cohabit with kites, and people with the spirits of the mountain.

The Maenllwyd was bought by my Buddhist teacher John Crook in 1975, as a place to hold Buddhist retreats. It has been serving as a retreat centre ever since, and is also used by his family for holidays. People who went on early retreats with John talk with nostalgia about how, in the early days, everything took place in the small, cottagey house. People washed themselves in the stream, and the sleeping quarters became the meditation room during the day. The morning boards were struck to wake them up at

4 am instead of today's 5. Even today there is no electricity; it is heated by wood fires and lit by candles and paraffin lamps. Sleeping accommodation is basic, and retreatants sleep on simple futons in dormitories. It isn't a large place; it accommodates barely twenty people.

It melts each person that visits. It hooks them, it changes them. That is why John insisted on leaving the house in a basic state. The lack of electricity gives room to a different power to be active in the place. The inside is as noble and wild as the outside. The Maenllwyd has grown over time. Several years ago, one of the old farm buildings, just across the yard from the main house, was converted into a Chan Hall, where the main part of the retreats now takes place: silent meditation, chanting, talks and mindful communication exercises. There is an altar at one end, and a wood-burning stove at the other. In the winter, the Chan Hall is the warmest place.

John had spent the late sixties in California, where he had attended "Enlightenment Intensives"; a process invented by Charles Berner. It was based on Zen principles, but adapted to a secular, non-Buddhist context. John "re-consecrated" this approach, integrating it back into a traditional Zen Buddhist format and adding meditation, thereby creating the "Western Zen Retreat", which was first offered at the Maenllwyd in the mid 1970s. In these retreats, participants sit across from each other, asking one another a question such as "Tell me who you are" or "Tell me what love is" and listening in silence as their companion shares their inner world of thoughts and feelings, gradually unpacking fixed beliefs and stories, and letting them go. Many of the stories that I share in these pages come from these retreats.

John later met and became a student of Chan Master Sheng Yen, the Abbot of Dharma Drum Mountain Buddhist Monastery in Taiwan. Chan is the Chinese ancestor of Zen Buddhism. Chan, like Zen, means *dhyana*, or meditation, and the words Chan and Zen can, at least for the purposes of this book, be used interchangeably. In time, John became Sheng Yen's first lay (which means non-monastic) Dharma Heir, authorised to teach Chan in the West, and in 1997, he and others founded the Western Chan Fellowship (WCF)[1], an organisation dedicated to furthering the practice of Chan

---

1 www.westernchanfellowship.org

Buddhism. John continued to lead retreats at the Maenllwyd, and at other retreat centres, until his death in 2011, through both the original Western Zen Retreats and more traditional Chan retreats. Now Simon Child, who also received transmission from Master Sheng Yen and is a Dharma Heir, has succeeded John as the Teacher of the WCF. The retreats continue at the Maenllwyd and at other venues, under the guidance and teaching of Simon, and of the other retreat leaders trained by him and John.

John was a knowledgeable and enthusiastic bird watcher and ethologist. He studied bird and primate behaviour and made several expeditions to the Ladhaki and Tibetan mountains, researching the hermits and yogins who retreat in the caves and hermitages of the Himalayas. It was here that he received permission to teach the Tibetan *Mahamudra* practice, which I write about in Chapter 16. When I first met him he used to intimidate me; there was a severity in his gaze, a "nowhere to hide" feeling around him. Over the years I came to love him. He was an inspiring, charismatic teacher with deep warmth and compassion. He was a shaman, a man of science and of Zen, who also had room for the more esoteric elements of Tibetan Buddhism. It was through his stories, his rituals and his openness that I began to connect with the wild of the place, to the wild in myself.

On retreats, the teacher offers instruction and one-to-one interviews to all the retreatants, but he or she is not the only important person. Hospitality and taking care are paramount, and this is where the Guestmaster comes in. He or she is responsible for the day-to-day well-being of the retreatants, and for the management of the work periods: twice a day, everyone takes on their share of work, in the garden, the Chan Hall, or in the kitchen. The Guestmaster is the timekeeper, waking everyone at 5am and marking the end of each work period with a pair of wooden clappers. He or she also keeps order in the Chan Hall and acts as stage manager for any events. The Guestmaster works closely with the cook and each uses their role as Zen practice.

The tradition of the Zen cook, or *Tenzo*, is an ancient one. The thirteenth century Zen Master, Dogen, wrote his *Instructions to a Zen Cook* in 1237. Zen cooking is the meditative practice of preparing food for others, with focus, awareness and above all, with heart, creating meals that nourish and comfort people who are taking part in Buddhist retreats. The cook lies at the heart of the community. In Zen Buddhism, preparing and eating food are a very important part of training, of spiritual practice. You cultivate awareness and gratitude towards the efforts of everybody and everything that has contributed to the growing and the cooking of the meal.

Zen cooking is as much a state of being as of doing. It is intuitive. The cook's practice is entirely aligned to the needs of others. The cook works towards losing the small self within the flow of the moment, towards becoming one with the space and the ingredients, the elements and the environment.

The kitchen has been modernised since I began to cook in the Maenllwyd, but it remains rustic, almost precarious, given the amount of cooking that needs to be done on a retreat. No electricity means no fridge and no food processors; to me, that is the best part. The Maenllwyd kitchen is an organic space that enables the creative and artistic process of cooking to take place.

There is a well-stocked pantry or back kitchen, which leads out onto a back yard; a short walk up the garden takes you to Green Tara, a statue of a Tibetan Buddhist deity, who represents compassion in action. One of the traditional stories claims that she was formed from a single teardrop, shed by another Buddhist deity, *Avalokiteshvara*, when he saw the enormous scale of pain and suffering of the world and realised that he could not possibly appease it. Tara has an important place in this story; it is by her statue that I, in accordance with Buddhist tradition, leave a food offering, or *puja*, taken from every meal we eat. In Buddhism a puja is a ritual, an offering ceremony performed as an act of honour, worship or gratitude.

After the mealtime grace with which we start every meal, the teacher serves Tara first, with a small portion of each dish served in tiny stainless steel bowls on a tray which is then taken out into the garden and offered at the feet of her statue.

Three times a day, animals feast on these little dishes of food. Tiny, winged bugs and black, shiny slugs, ladybirds, crawling creatures. Over time, I began to notice their beauty and made sure I checked the bowls when I collected them from Tara. The bowl of soup often had drowning casualties, mostly slugs. This saddened me. How could I protect them? On one of my earliest retreats, I took with me a bunch of Thai orchids, which I placed on the windowsill in the kitchen, picking one flower to adorn the tray of offerings from each meal. The orchids left on Tara's steps were devoured by the slugs; I felt sure that feasting on the orchids distracted the slugs from falling into the liquid. So flowers began to accompany the food, as a part of each offering, and the slugs loved them. Without making a conscious decision to do so, I had begun to care for the slugs, and feeding them flowers was a way of loving them. It was also a good way to look after love itself, something I had failed at so many times.

A friend who worked with me in the kitchen and who observed this ritual said that if I ever wrote a book, I should call it *Feeding Orchids to the Slugs*. Slugs have played a pivotal role in the restoration of my relationship with things around me; I have learned to notice the splendour of life even in the slimiest of creatures. I have found beauty in what I used to perceive as ugly. Slowly I have learned to love that which is difficult to love, both in myself and in others.

Some people have responded negatively when I have mentioned the title: "How disgusting." "I really don't like slugs." "You can't publish a book about food and cooking, with slugs in the title!" Yet I felt very strongly that the title had to remain. Zen is expansive and all encompassing, and sometimes we may have to experience discomfort in order to get to the beauty of being itself.

Chapter Two
Retreat One: *The Little Girl*

Notice how the truth tends to manifest

Unexpectedly

In the small things we are often too drowsy to see

In constant whispers we are often too busy to hear...

I was thirty-five when I went on my first retreat. My husband Simon booked me a place, as a birthday present. He had gone on retreat whilst I was away in Argentina with our children, and came back ecstatic, full of stories, having had a powerful experience.

I was in two minds whether I wanted to go. Simon had been a practising Buddhist for years, and I often resented his practice. I felt like it separated us. I wasn't looking for a religion and the idea of spending nearly a week in silence, meditating, seemed like a daunting task rather than something to look forward to. Why didn't he buy me a spa day? I had two young children; going away for five days felt impossibly self-indulgent.

The date approached and although I was too shy to cancel it, I felt anxious, grumpy, exceedingly nervous and quite unwilling to go. I felt resentful, as if I was being sent away to be indoctrinated in a practice I had little interest in. In spite of this I borrowed some wellington boots and packed a small bag with comfortable clothes, warm vests and a torch. Along with all the negative feelings, I was aware that life had been difficult during the past few years, and that I needed a break. I wanted to get to the bottom of a deep-rooted unhappiness in my life, a void that seemed to suck me in, a dark whirlpool of sadness, homesickness and longing.

I arrived at the Maenllwyd a tired, battered, sad person, my back and fists tensed to a knot, feeling unprepared, unready, reluctant, my overcrowded mind holding on to threads. We were met by the Guestmaster, a kind, tall man who carried my bag all the way up a narrow metal staircase, to the mezzanine communal bedroom above the Chan Hall. A converted barn with exposed beams and limewashed walls, the room was warm and welcoming.

I crossed the yard to the house where I poured myself a cup of tea and found a place on one of the sitting room's sofas. The blazing fire embraced a group of strangers. Simon Child, the teacher, welcomed us. The house was rudimentary, bucolic and drafty, it had no electricity, but paraffin lamps and candles made the room glow.

When I went to bed I made a commitment to work hard at making this retreat work for me. In the morning we were to be allocated our jobs for the two daily work periods that form a component of the retreats: there is an old Zen adage that says "no work, no food". For some reason I had a strong desire to work in the kitchen. Something was calling me there to learn something new, something about myself.

Five o'clock the following morning, I was up and dressed. We gathered in the yard to do some simple physical exercises - I enjoyed them, I felt so much beauty in the air. Yet I could hardly bend over; every muscle in my body was rigid. We had tea and then did a thirty minute meditation sitting; I struggled with this sitting, having no idea what to do, but I persisted and it eventually came to an end.

It was still early in the morning when I had my first interview with Simon. He told me that the desire to find out who I am put me on the right track. I felt slightly defensive but I trusted him. I told him I was prepared to dig deep, as I felt I was destroying myself with the negative, habitual patterns that I didn't seem able to escape. He gave me my question which I was to work with on this retreat: "Tell me who you are." I told him that I was prepared to cry; that I had brought lots of tissues. He seemed happy with my approach. For once, I didn't attempt to trick him. I didn't try and show him that actually I thought I had it all sussed out.

Breakfast was at seven. The silence was maintained at all times, even during meals. To mark the start of each meal, Simon knocked two stones together three times, and we recited a grace from a laminated card in front of us.

> At one with the food we eat,
> We identify with the universe.
> At one with the universe,
> We taste the food.
> The universe and the food we eat
> Partake of the same nature.
> We share the merits of this food with all.
> The first bite is to discard evil.
> The second bite is to train in perfection.
> The third bite is to help all beings.
> We pray that all may be enlightened.

I was captivated by the grace, but had been awake for hours and was ready for sleep. I could hear all sorts of noises coming from people's bodies, and from my own. Someone slurped his tea quite loudly. I drank green tea and ate the porridge and a piece of bread with a thick layer of honey. I was the only one not finishing the porridge. I didn't like it.

The words from the grace kept resonating as I savoured the food. I was moved by the solemnity of the silent, contemplative nature of the meal.

After breakfast came a work period, but first we washed our crockery and cutlery whilst sitting at the table, passing hot kettles from person to person, pouring hot water into our bowl and mug and washing the smudges of leftover food with our cutlery. We then dried each item with a piece of kitchen towel. I immediately loved the ceremonial silence and the clanking sounds of the dishes. People looked tired, apprehensive, self-conscious. When everyone had finished and total silence had fallen again, Simon knocked the two stones together and we recited the end of meal grace:

The universe is as the boundless sky.

As lotus blossoms above unclean water,

Pure and beyond the world is the mind of the trainee.

Oh silence of nature

We take refuge in thee.

We vow to deliver innumerable sentient beings.

We vow to cut off endless vexations.

We vow to master limitless approaches to Dharma.

We vow to attain supreme Buddhahood.

The teacher gave instructions for the work period and allocated each person a job. As I was hoping, I was going to work in the kitchen.

The kitchen has a primitive, powerful and enchanting presence. The anteroom with an external door forms a rough-hewn, whitewashed cavern of a pantry in which boxes and sacks of produce lie waiting for use. As there is no electric lighting everything dances in light and shadow thrown by the kerosene lamps. Just inside the door between pantry and kitchen is the glowing heart of the house, a white Rayburn stove that feeds on lumps of coal and produces vast amounts of ash, which I watch being emptied and carried through the pantry and outside in a metal bucket. The Rayburn exudes heat and comfort in the kitchen, but is temperamental unless you treat her right. At that moment I had no idea how close and intimate she and I would become, and how reflective of one another's inner workings.

The cook, Miche, showed me how to prepare the cheese plates for lunch. This was to be my daily job. The cheese was kept in a 1950s metal larder box, with mesh to keep out the flies. I went into the garden at the back to pick some nasturtiums to decorate the plates. The back garden, flanked by a tumbling mountain stream, leads onto the steep edge of the mountain. Just outside the door is a clump of three ancient-looking sycamores, with knotted bark faces like mountain trolls, and just beyond them on a small mound is a statue of Green Tara, the goddess of compassion. This was my first ever encounter with Tara.

The cheese was not my only task. We chopped and stirred onions in a giant wok, we helped to mix the cake. Miche was giving instruction after instruction, and it felt a bit frantic. We missed our break, as we didn't hear the wooden clappers announcing the end of the work period. I felt so tired I could weep.

I found it hard to stay awake for Simon's daily dharma talk, which usually follows the morning's rest period, at around nine o'clock. I had had no rest following the extended work period. I kept telling myself: "Wake Up! You are always asleep, wake up!" He talked about what to do when thoughts arise in our mind: "Let them through, let them be, let them go".

I started to look forward to the clongs and clangs of the different bells and bowls, and to the knocking of the wooden fish, a percussion instrument used to keep the rhythm during the chanting of *sutras*, or Buddhist verses. They were beginning to awaken a part of me that had been dormant for a lifetime. I was struggling with my sitting meditation position. I was aching everywhere. I asked the Guestmaster for help. One of the participants happened to be a chiropractor, and quickly sorted my back. I felt brand new, and immensely grateful.

Slowly, I began to enjoy the reflective silence creating a space into which things generally obscured by the bustle of thought and conversation slowly emerged. Mostly though, what emerged was the chaos and confusion of my thoughts. Lots of images came into my mind, relating to my past. Thousands of other thoughts and images arose, mostly uninvited, in an agitated stream of consciousness. I was shocked at how fuzzy my mind was. All I heard was noise, nothing made sense.

Silence was beginning to force me to see my habitual responses to the world around me, to reflect on my instinctual reactions. I was beginning to feel exposed and vulnerable with all these strangers around me, without being able to tell them who I am, what I do, where I come from. Instead, I just had to be with me, whatever "me" was. "Tell me who you are."

Every afternoon before tea, we went for a walk. I walked up the hill, although I noticed that what I really wanted was to go down the hill and sit in a small copse of pine trees by the side of the road. I had noticed this wood as we drove up the track and felt a gentle nudge inside, a reminder of something from my childhood in Argentina perhaps. As I pushed on, up the steep slope, panting, I began to wonder why I didn't turn back around and go to the copse. I sensed a tingle of fear.

Halfway up the hill, I sat on the edge of the road to look at the view. I picked the wrong spot, and sat down right in front of a big sycamore tree, which meant I couldn't see the view. I looked at the bark of the tree. It was worn, brown and cracked into patterns born from its life experience. It would not have been much of an effort to move, to shift my body in order to see the valley below, the patchwork of fields and farms, the wind turbines far to my left, but I didn't. I just sat and gazed through the trunk. I recalled past events that haunted me. Nothing new, because I had seen them before, dealt with them in therapy, believed I had laid them to rest, but they keep coming back to me. I realised that I had been unable to let go of them because I had become used to them being there. I had made them too comfortable. What would I be without them? I realised that the ghosts in my mind were not ethereal; they were like the tree, so real. I kept asking myself the question: "Tell me who you are." The answer: "I am quite comfortable with not being able to see who I am, and instead I see through the tree ghosts in me, and focus on them, analyze their bark patterns, meanwhile I am missing out on the view, the big picture."

The valley was breathtakingly beautiful. If only I could be bothered to shift my body away from the tree to get the view at its best.

As I walked down the road, I saw a bunch of red berries in front of me, by my feet. I picked it up as if I was holding my burden, recalling the feelings, one by one. I told myself that I needed to throw the feelings away, so I hurled the berries with all my might. I kept walking, but there were the berries again. I have never been very good at throwing.

I picked up the berries once more, went through the gate into the farmyard and heard the stream. The sound of water soothed me. It occurred to me that I actually needed to see the berries floating away. So I set them free, one by one, each symbolizing a sorrow, and I watched them disappear downstream, with the gentle soundtrack of the stream in my ears.

The following work period I was back in the kitchen. Miche reminded me of a hummingbird, moving around the house carrying pots and dishes, serving meals with graceful confidence. I sat opposite her at the table, and watched her eat, laughing as she added things to her plate. When she ate, it was as if she was dancing with the food.

I enjoyed learning the principles behind the chopping of each different vegetable. She told us about "the yin and yang of an onion", how to slice it following the natural lines of each half, according to macrobiotic principles. How thick should it be? Did you know that you can keep tears to a minimum by leaving the root untouched until the very end? The pantry was piled with stacks of blue mushroom crates filled with seasonal, organic vegetables, with metal bins and tubs full of grains and nuts and flours. I found that I moved in the kitchen with great ease. I was already a confident cook but I was here to put my head down, to do what I was told. Secretly I was watching what everyone was doing, which is the way I learn best: watching.

I loved the sense of community when we were all at work: people washing up, making bread, topping up the coal, chopping wood, cleaning the house, filling paraffin lamps. The silence made it peculiarly compelling, indeed beautiful: each person paying full attention to their task.

During the rest period, I sat by the window on my bed. There was a warm summery breeze, an autumnal feel of burning wood and melancholic Sunday afternoons in Argentina. My mind turned to my migraines and the way I have always used food against myself, as a punishment rather than as nourishment. I had always thought that I cooked with love, yet I suddenly realised that I was unable to love myself through food. I asked Simon if I could have an interview with Miche. I assured him it was relevant to my question. I didn't want to ask about recipes, or anything specific. It felt more of a call, a call to the kitchen, a deep fascination with the tiny, quaint space, as if the space itself was guarding a secret I wanted to know.

The interview went well. She too grew up in warmer climates, with lighter food. We talked about the importance of relearning that food can be a healer. We discussed intuition and nurturing, how to listen to our body's needs before we prepare our food.

Afterwards I felt happy. Something had shifted in me. Perhaps I had begun to connect in a deeper way with my body as I had always connected with my mind. How could I be kinder to myself, mind and body? Could I learn to use food as a communion, a form of connection? Could cooking become a creative process that would allow this to happen?

It was time to walk again. I wanted to go to the wood, but instead I turned into a field on my left and sat there for a while. Although I looked, I could not see the wood. I wanted to ask someone to come with me, but I had taken a vow of silence. Perhaps I could ask Simon.

We did a session of moving meditation, where we shook and danced to music, followed by half an hour lying or sitting on the floor. Although I managed to let my body go with the music, I didn't feel sensual. I felt unconnected to myself, a long-held habit, I suddenly realised. I longed for connection, and cried throughout the dance.

During the next dharma talk, Simon spoke about living a lie. This resonated deeply with me, and in our next interview, I told him how I yearned to find HOME, that I felt split and uncomfortable everywhere, ill at ease with myself. Together we explored my need to find a home within me, so that I could be happy anywhere. I needed to stop looking for the ideal place. Like the snail, I needed to learn to love my home, to be home, to carry it with me wherever I go.

After a communication exercise, where we worked in pairs with our questions, I went outside for a break and ate an apple. It tasted so good that I ate it all: core, seeds, the lot. I felt sensual as I ate it; so did the apple. Eating the apple, including the chewy bits and the seeds, felt like accepting and loving all of me, including all the things I dislike. Like the forbidden fruit that hides a secret, each bite led into a profound awareness, like biting a chunk of self-knowledge.

Things were beginning to make sense. I began to feel more open to shifts and changes. I caught the copse in the corner of my eye and I felt scared, why can't I go there? Later, while meditating, it occurred to me that the copse merely represented somewhere I would like to go to, something I would like to do, that I feel that I can't. I recognised a destructive pattern, the one that made me feel constantly unfulfilled. The only thing stopping me from going to the woods was myself.

I was enjoying the communication exercises but each time, when it came to choosing a partner, I feared that no one would pick me. Why would someone pick me?

The retreat was halfway through, and I was still avoiding the woods. I told Simon and he suggested that I go to the woods instead of going to meditation.

And so I went. As I went through the gate into the small copse I felt immediately transported, playful. I saw an image of me as a little girl, and sensed a time when I used to feel lovely and nice, when nothing was wrong, a time when I was happy and connected to everything and everyone around me. I must have been seven or eight.

As if watching a film, I moved to a forgotten scene of my childhood. I was in Hosteria Las Vertientes, a beautiful old place in my grandma's village. It had a big pool surrounded by pine trees and picnic tables. You could pay for the day to use the pool and we used to take picnics. We used to go with my extended family, who spent their summers in the village. Perhaps the smell of pine needles and lichen awakened the memory in me. I am with a crew of cousins playing by the side of the pool. We swim, we play games, we read comics. One of my cousins, the one I feel closest to, says:

"I'm thirsty, let's go and buy coke!"

We all loved the alluring little glass bottles of Coca-Cola, chilled to perfection, which came with a stripy straw.

"Yes, let's go," I said.

His response came into my memory like a blow. "You are not coming," he said.

"Why not?" I asked, curious at his sudden rejection. After all, he almost feels like my brother.

"Because you are ugly, fat, poor and you don't belong with us."

Nobody disagreed with him. Instead they giggled. I can remember standing there, taking the blow, believing what he had just said. I can recall the shock, seeing them all run to their parents to raid their purses.

Sitting, now, in the wood, I am wrapped in the same pain I felt then. The pain sunk me down into the concrete surrounding the pool. I told no-one about it.

I had completely forgotten this incident. Sitting there in the wood, I realised that the girl who was told that she didn't belong, that she was ugly, fat and poor, still lives inside me. The memory arose from the sense of place, from the smell of pine needles, from the touch of bark while sitting on a fallen tree. As in the episode of the madeleine, described by Proust in *In Search of Lost Time*, involuntary memories of things long forgotten and buried are awakened by sensory experiences that transport us to specific moments of our past. Perhaps this explained why I was struggling to answer my question: "Tell me who you are." In order to answer the question fully I needed to peel away the layers of events that shaped the person that I am today.

As I sat in the little forest I realised there was nothing dark or sinister about the place. I listened to the wind and felt the moist air in my face. Why had it taken me so long to get here? The gates were easy to open; there was a tiny creek to cross, but I had wellies so it wasn't a big deal. The little girl in me was pleading with me to bring her, she needed me to remember the damaging words, change the context, help her heal, change the mirror. I saw myself in the woods of Ongamira, another wild playground of my childhood, a younger me, smiling, surrounded by friends and family. I was beginning to understand what needs to be healed. I needed to start with the girl, place her in a meadow of flowers, in the magic woods. I needed to let the woman in me be.

I continued to feel vulnerable. Every time we had to choose a partner, every time I sat at the table, I noticed the same thought, that nobody liked me, why would they like me? I told Simon about the moment in the woods, about the memories of what my cousin had said to me that sunny afternoon, and how it became the only truth that defined me. Simon worked very hard at guiding me on the right path. It was hard to go back to painful places but when I did I was so happy and relieved. What I encountered was a cute eight year old Flor with honey coloured hair who believed she was beautiful and smart and happy, a Flor who was good at most things, Flor the artistic one, Flor the writer.

I needed to feel beautiful, I needed to open up.

On the fourth day, as I ate my lunch in silence surrounded by strangers, I bit into a chunky soup and in that moment, the second between chewing and the food moving upwards towards my palate, something imploded, as if I was tasting food for the first time. For a second, that carrot was everything. Although I have eaten carrots nearly every day of my life, this was about something completely different, this was about being at one with the food we eat, like in the grace. Something happened during that bite, like an implosion of knowledge that connected me with everything, like a flicker of a moment that lasted an eternity. The carrot tasted like nothing I have ever tasted because I don't think I had ever truly tasted food before that moment. Everything I needed to know was in that bite and as I swallowed it, I felt like weeping, knowing that the next chunk of carrot was not going to have the same effect.

It was a wake-up call, an awakening of something that was in me, dormant, hiding underneath all the self preoccupation. I looked for that experience in each mouthful of food afterwards.

I made this drawing in my notebook. At the end of the retreat, I felt more Flower, I felt like the Flor I used to know (Flor means flower in Spanish, and was always my pet name before I came to England).

before   after

It felt like moving from a haunted house to an airy and light place with ample rooms and big windows. Some of my pictures were still on the walls, but they were scattered and well placed.

In the last dance, I danced with that eight year old me, the one that believed she could do anything, the one that felt beautiful. I danced with my friend Mandeep, who always sees that little girl in me. I was struck by how beautiful everyone looked. Had my face gone through that transformation? Their exuberant radiance, so different from the faces of the first day, reflected just how I was feeling inside.

I needed to return to this place, and the call was from the kitchen. Somehow I knew, in a very instinctual, wild sense, that the kitchen, the practice in it, the sacredness of the space could help me to reveal some more memories, to reconnect me with this "me" that I had lost on the way. The kitchen had heart, and its simplicity held a promise to connect me with all things.

Before I left I told Simon that I wanted to train as a cook. He said he would be in touch. Miche gave me a card that I framed, and hung above the white Rayburn at home. It is a saying from the *Upanishads*: "First know food. From food all things are born, by food they live, toward food they move, into food they return."

Chapter Three

Storms and Siestas

My personal journey as a cook started in my childhood. I grew up around stock pots, fresh warm bread, and seasonal vegetables from the market on Tuesdays. I used to watch fresh pasta being rolled out by the women in the family, and enjoyed the meat feast barbecues, skilfully tended by the men. Most of the major events of my life have been connected with food and as I embarked on my voyage of self-confrontation, the events of my past unfolded, their emotional residue intact, with all the flavours of the times.

Something about the kitchen at the Maenllwyd transported me to my childhood in Argentina, especially to the house in the hills where my maternal grandparents lived, where I spent my weekends and long summer holidays.

The house in the hills had presence, a jolly spirited presence, with walls crawling with ivy, and airy conservatories. Set in the middle of expansive wooded grounds, it was long and divided in three. Attached to one side of the house, there was the general store that my grandparents ran, the bakery and a series of outbuildings. On the other side, there was a big patio with a long table, and a formal garden that my grandmother tended passionately whenever she had a spare moment. We were often told to stay away from the general store side of the house if we were on our own, without an adult. Some of the bedroom windows faced that side and were sheltered by a vigorous vine.

Rich images of the life I lived there ebb and flow when I am in the Maenllwyd, like invisible silk ribbons dangling from the ceiling.

The house was lively, always busy. The only quiet periods were after lunch, when we took our siesta. The men in the house rose at two in the morning to begin baking, so this was a sacred rest.

Although now I see siestas as contemplative times that we were lucky to have, as kids we hated that time of day. We got bored. We had to entertain ourselves and we had to hush and tip toe, as we needed to be unheard, silent.

If we were lucky, we were allowed to stay out, under the shade of trees, playing in hush-hush tones. We invented games, pastimes. We played cards and constructed dens under the pine trees. Sometimes we collected wild flowers to make perfume in small medicine bottles and built apothecaries and pharmacies. One hot afternoon, plagued by the sound of cicadas, I got tired of having to do things in a hush, so I decided to rebel against the siesta, and not to rest. I wandered around the house and went outside, losing track of time, going through the door of the laundry room, through the bakery and coming out on the other side. I was scared I was in trouble. I was on the wrong side of the house, and I ended up outside my grandparents' bedroom.

The garden looked different, less cluttered. Someone must have removed the crates with the empty soda siphon bottles because this is where they were always kept, hiding away, waiting to be taken to be refilled. It was a shame because I liked rearranging all the glass bottles by their different shades of blue and green. It would have given me something to do. Some of the hens were rooting around for insects. I hoped the vicious cockerel had not escaped. He was so bad-tempered he kept pecking people; now he was kept in isolation.

My mum's favourite chair had been brought here for some reason. It was an old French garden chair, the flaked sage paint peeling off its legs. It was leaning against the wooden shutters of the bedroom window. My grandparents' bedroom was the coolest room of the house in summer. It was south-facing, sheltered by the pergola wrapped in vine leaves and ripe, violet grapes that we were saving for my grandma, for her grappa. I stood under the structure's dense shade, which swathed me abruptly in a chilly wave, tickling my bare arms with a cool tinge. It was swift and didn't last long, but it was enough to make me sneeze. I looked up and closed my eyes as a few hot rays of sun managed to filter through the gaps left by the latest hailstorm.

The summer months used to bring spectacular electric storms. Since the terrain was mountainous, we were always at risk of flash floods. We used to be taken out of the water, if we were in the pool, and brought indoors. We used to watch as the grown-ups silently began to close all the shutters and draw the curtains. There was an air of excitement, of anticipation, of fear. We used to watch it all from the kitchen window, because it had a metallic mosquito mesh on it, so even if the hail broke the glass we were protected. The fifth storm since Spring had brought a bombardment of hailstones the size of tennis balls, first coming almost horizontally into the house, then, as the wind changed, freefalling at a terrifying speed, ripping and smashing anything in their way, rapidly covering the ground with a blanket of ice. That storm had broken every single glass pane in the sunroom.

The stones were so big that we later found dozens of dead green parrots and other birds in the grounds of the house. They had been ripped from their nests by an avalanche of hail. We spent the rest of the afternoon digging burial grounds and making crosses with twigs, laying them to rest in mass graves.

After that storm I knew that when the sky darkened in the middle of a hot day, it meant trouble. The atmosphere grew dense, and the electricity went off. My grandmother used to say that she felt it in her skin and in all her scars. She grew up in a farm and was hardly ever wrong about the weather. She could read the colour of the sky.

Everyone was asleep and I could hear my grandfather snoring in the bedroom. I was surrounded by silence; not a pin dropped. The cat had disappeared as he did every day and even the dogs were snoozing. I felt like eating something sweet but the shop's back door had been locked. Grandad always used to pull the metal shutter halfway down after lunch, so that people didn't come to the back of the house with requests, clapping their hands, expecting to be served.

I used to love being in the store. Often I was allowed behind the counter if the shop was not too busy. I used to help sell sweets and espadrilles, but I was the best at selling biscuits, which were sold by the kilo and kept in big, metal tins with glass windows. Everyone used to say that I was a biscuit expert, a *galletitologa especialista*. I could sell my favourite biscuits with a passion.

I noticed that the grapes on the pergola were hanging too high, but that some might be reachable.

Maybe I could bring a ladder, but instead I placed the old French chair by the wall and aimed for a lower bunch that did not look too high up. It was nearer one of the gaps in the foliage, where the light could reach, and the sun had made it ripen faster than the rest. Some of the grapes at the top of the bunch were beginning to wrinkle. I snapped the bunch of grapes from the vine and as I stood on tiptoe on the chair, a sudden hot draught from the north wind lifted up my cotton dress and the air ran through my legs. I sat on the chair and started sucking on the grapes. The skin was tough and there were far too many seeds yet the juice was sweet. I spat out the pips and the skin; I wanted to spit them as far as I could. I knew it was rude, but that my grandmother would laugh about it. My mother would definitely tell me off. I was getting good at spitting and my cousin Tomas was teaching me to whistle like a boy.

A fat fly appeared out of nowhere and sat on my lap. I shook it off but it came straight back. Perhaps some of the grape juice had spilled down my dress; maybe that was why it kept hovering around me. I took off the dress. I had my swimming costume on underneath, the blue one with polka dots. The fly soon lost interest in me. I was really hot and I wanted to swim. At that moment, siesta time felt the most boring thing in the whole world. I wasn't allowed to go to the swimming pool on my own.

I heard a noise in the kitchen: perhaps my grandmother had woken up. She had promised to make *Islas Flotantes* for dessert that evening. There would be jobs to do: we would have to collect the eggs from the pen and I would help her divide the whites from the yolk and beat them until they were fluffy and spongy.

I put my dress back on, glad that I was no longer the only one awake.

Islas flotantes de Serafina

Serves 6

For the islas:
  6 egg whites
  A tiny squeeze of lemon juice
  120 g caster sugar
  1 litre full-fat milk
  2 tsp vanilla essence
  (You could use vanilla sugar instead. At home I keep a jar of caster sugar with vanilla pods.)

For the crème anglaise:
  10 egg yolks
  80 g caster sugar

For the caramel:
  150 ml water
  300 g caster sugar

For the islas you are basically making a meringue, so whisk the egg whites and lemon juice in a clean bowl until soft peaks form when you take away the whisk. Add the sugar a little at a time whilst continuing to whisk, until stiff peaks form when you lift the whisk.

Boil some water. Bring the milk and the vanilla essence to the boil in the largest pan you own. Once it has boiled, reduce the heat and leave it to simmer. Make sure you have a lid for the pan.

Pour the boiling water into a bowl and dip two large spoons in it, then use the spoons to make the 8 mounds which are to become the islas. Use the spoons to give them shape. Carefully transfer each isla into the simmering milk and vanilla mix.

Cover the pan and poach the meringue islas for 8-10 minutes, remembering to gently turn them over after a few minutes so that they cook evenly.

Using a metal slotted spoon, and being extremely careful, take out the islas and set them aside on a tray. Do not remove the milk from the simmering heat.

For the crème anglaise, whisk the egg yolks and caster sugar together in a mixing bowl, until the mixture is smooth and the sugar has dissolved.

Steadily add the hot milk to the egg yolk and sugar mixture, never ceasing to whisk. When you have mixed it all together, transfer it back into the pan and turn the heat to medium. Take a wooden spoon and mix constantly, until the custard has thickened. Pour the custard into a large bowl and place it over some cold water: ideally the water should contain some ice cubes. Continue stirring from time to time to help it cool.

To make the caramel, pour the water and sugar into a thick-based pan and cook over moderate heat, stirring and making sure that the sugar has dissolved. Boil the mixture whilst stirring it until the colour changes and it becomes a dark golden-brown. Pour it into a flat serving tray with even sides, deep as a lasagne dish, and spread it evenly.

Transfer some of the cool custard into the tray, then float the islas evenly in it. Pour the rest of the custard around and slightly over them and chill.

Just before serving, dip the base of the tray into some warm water to melt the caramel slightly so that you can pour the juices over the islas as you serve them in individual bowls.

Chapter Four
Retreat Two: *Learning the Ropes*

To study the Way is to study the self.
To study the self is to forget the self.
To forget the self is to be enlightened
By all things of the universe.

~ Dogen

A few months after my first retreat, Miche invited me to join her on a summer retreat to train as a Tenzo. I was to receive training for the first few days, to get acquainted with the way things were done, and then I would be left to cook by myself for the last two days. I accepted with gratitude and without hesitation.

I met Miche in a nearby village, where she took me to meet the local farmer, Evan, and collect the produce she had ordered from him. He loaded boxes of fresh vegetables into my car. We visited the local wholefood shop to collect last minute sundries and then began the long drive up the track. As we arrived at the house, I felt an immediate and comforting sense of home. I walked into the kitchen and knew I was where I longed to be.

I had learned during my first retreat that, since leaving Argentina in my twenties, I had struggled with a deep feeling of homelessness. Home was a scatter of places in which I had lived but none had made me feel grounded. For the past twenty years I had been harking back to some ideal place which didn't exist anymore. What was it in that kitchen that called me so much, pulled me towards her, invited me in whispers?

I could not wait to be left on my own, to experience the space alone, but there was so much that needed to be learnt.

I knew nobody apart from Miche. The teacher was a Welshman called Ken Jones, who welcomed us warmly. The retreat was based around the teachings of the Japanese Zen teacher, Dogen, who based his extensive *Instructions to the Zen Cook* around his experiences of visiting Chinese monasteries in the thirteenth century.

We set the tables and got the kitchen going, unpacking the boxes of produce and putting things away. I listened attentively. I was there to learn, and to begin to relate to the space and the practice. I took my rests in the field by the Chan Hall, with the sheep. I lay on a blanket, soaking up the sunshine and the sounds of nature, embraced by the landscape.

Miche showed me the basic procedures and talked about the importance of good timekeeping. There was so much information to retain. We joined the other retreatants in the Chan Hall whenever we could; Ken's dharma talks were inspirational. I soaked up all the instructions: from Miche, from Ken and from Dogen. I observed Miche as she instructed the kitchen team; I watched as the metal bowls filled up with carefully chopped and sliced vegetables; I learned how to "riddle" the Rayburn, a process of agitating the coals to release ash, and how to plan the cooking around her variable heat. There was a strong sense of splendour in the simplest of tasks.

Ken told us to stop thinking about time as separate from ourselves: you are time just as much as you are your body and you are your emotions. We tweaked soups and I observed how meals arose out of pure inspiration: there were no set methods or recipes. Dogen counselled letting go of planning in order to relate to the kitchen, to the ingredients, to the retreatants, and to yourself. Miche shared her artistic style of cooking with me, and little by little, I was left alone to prepare food myself.

Miche asked me to make a cake. There were no books, no recipes, no wheat or any sugar. She gave me one egg. She wanted to show me how to trust the process and be creative. One part of me was terrified of making a mess of it, another rose up to the challenge. "Create!" she said, "The Zen Kitchen is all about trust." So I experimented. I set about the making of the cake in the same way as I would start a thirty minute meditation session. It is impossible to begin a period of meditation knowing exactly what the outcome will be. I gathered all the ingredients, breathed and started. I had no clue if it would work. I made a pear, elderflower and polenta cake, which was firm and moist, golden, tasty.

As planned, Miche left the retreat two days before it ended, and I was left as the cook. She left me with a box with all the remaining vegetables and a few ingredients. She said that the rest of the pantry was out of reach; she had done a stock take and asked me not to use anything else. I found this to be the biggest teaching. A part of me wanted to impress, and I felt hard done by: the meagre box gave me no choice or control. Soon I realised that I needed to drop the negativity, and just cook, allowing the ingredients to impress instead. Working to bring the best out of the ingredients became a mirror: just as I tried to bring the best out of myself for the benefit of others. Everything I cooked tasted as it should, and the retreatants confirmed this by leaving only crumbs on their plates.

Ken gave an inspiring talk in which he said that Zen practice was about making your life into a work of art.

I decided to make a curry before I noticed that there were hardly any spices in the jars above the sink. It tasted good anyway: unusual, if mild.

Ken left everybody meditating in the Chan Hall and came to the kitchen to help me. He told me that Dogen observed that in Chinese monasteries, the cook, or Tenzo, was chosen because of their "way-seeking mind". What was the meaning of the "way-seeking mind"? What was I seeking?

I washed up and Ken dried as we continued talking about the meaning of being time whilst the rice cooked.

On the last afternoon, I returned to the pine tree copse, and to the memories that had awakened on my first retreat. Somehow the kitchen and the creative element of cooking were in that place, and training as Tenzo was the first step in a long journey ahead: a chosen path, or a path that chose me.

We finished the retreat with a walk up the stream. Ken led a fire puja, a ritual of offering up or letting go, on a big rock by the water. We built a pyre with pebbles and wood, and chanted as we watched the fire burn. Deep in the crevice of the mountain, by a beautiful pool of water, my heart swelled with gratitude for that moment, for finding a home, *cartref*, in the grey rock. *Cartref yn y Maenllwyd.*

In the autumn I trained with Pam, who was the cooks' coordinator and a highly experienced Tenzo. Her approach was radically different, and the retreat we were sharing was double in size. John Crook, the founder of the

Western Chan Fellowship, was leading the retreat. It was my first encounter with John and I felt slightly nervous about the whole thing.

Pam threw several different catastrophe scenarios at me: from burst pipes and cooking with no water from the tap, to blocked septic tanks or vegetables going off before you have had a chance to use them. She told me never to put food under a paraffin lamp, as they sometimes leak. She showed me how to do a stock take. She also tried (and failed) to teach me how to light the lamps. She had a different approach from Miche: she planned menus carefully, using Excel spreadsheets.

My body was tired and I gave myself a little question: "What is a cook?" I was beginning to wonder why I had opted for the kitchen rather than the meditation hall. What was this dormant cook aiming to achieve, apart from a sore back and exhaustion?

I rested very little but after the second day I felt energised, fully in my element. I learnt new things about the kitchen in a different season, like how to keep fires going. My timing improved, and I was able to experiment with my own recipes for the last two days. Pam left me to it and joined everyone else in the Chan Hall. I cooked and danced around the kitchen, never losing focus, continually learning the attention to detail which is needed for things to flow. I made a pledge that, as Tenzo, I was going to enjoy myself. In the act of nourishing and of learning to be fully present in each step, I would nurture my life and those around me. Some words from Ken's instructions during the summer retreat kept resonating in me: "Make your life a work of art." I sensed that I could begin this work in the tiny Maenllwyd kitchen.

On the last morning we burnt all the paper and the cardboard boxes on a big bonfire. Only a small pile of fruit was left from all our provisions: we offered it to the retreatants, for their journey home. The gradual emptying of the kitchen echoed my own sense of leaving my past stories behind. After that retreat, John and Pam judged me ready for the challenge of cooking a retreat on my own; my journey took on a different tone.

Chapter Five

Tara

Tara and I never had a proper introduction. On my first ever retreat, Miche asked me if I would like to take the offering to Tara. She handed me a metal tray with small stainless steel bowls containing the first servings of each dish, and an incense stick, and said:

"Take the tray through the kitchen, light the incense, wave it, blow out the candle on the windowsill and leave the offering on the steps outside doing your own ritual."

I was clueless about what I was doing. I had no ritual, no idea of what or who Tara was, but I enjoyed being asked, and going out and looking at the trees.

It was the same during the two retreats when I was training with other cooks. Each cook has their own practice and way of making offerings, so the basic ceremonial was explained more and less as yet one more task to add to the endless list of things to do.

I had decided, when I started training, to opt out of reading books about Zen. I wanted to dive into the practice without knowing what I was diving into. I wanted to approach the path without expectation.

So I didn't read anything about methods of practice, nor about Tara, although I did ask people about their experience of her.

To begin with, I resented the time spent taking the offering. It was yet another thing to juggle: having to collect the dishes from the previous meal's offering, whilst preparing the next. Yet at the same time, I was hearing from others about Tara being the guardian of the cooks, the helper, the active compassionate Buddha who came to aid the cooks in despair. I heard of floods of tears being shed on her steps, and of the strength she provided to others during the arduous hours of Tenzo practice.

The statue in the garden is emerald green and wears a crown. She has permanent, pen-painted eyes that look or stare, and she gets retouched each year as she sheds her skin, as the chalky Farrow and Ball paint starts to flake off. She is the Buddha of intuitive wisdom, and her aim is to bestow the highest happiness. Her left hand has the thumb and ring finger touching and holding the stem of a lotus flower, and her elbow is bent, so that her hand reaches up to her left shoulder. Her right hand is stretched out over the right knee with the palm facing down, which is the gesture of utmost generosity. She has a graceful posture: her right leg is outstretched and her left leg is pulled slightly towards her. This is what makes Green Tara active and agile, as she is sitting but not quite, ready to get up to help, prepared for swift action.

My Christian (protestant) upbringing made it difficult for me to connect to a statue, to ask something from a deity, and perhaps that is how I saw Tara for a while, as a statue that I felt I had to be grateful for, without knowing why. At first I felt very sceptical about it all, kneeling and asking, rubbing her knee as others had told me they did, but for some reason I continued to do it.

I began to cherish my Tara moments when I became aware that my way of looking at things shifted each time I went to the steps with my offering. There were simple things that happened whilst I was with Tara: face-to-face encounters with insects and animals; sudden glimpses of majestic red kites flying low, courting. Sometimes it was a rainbow, or the light at dusk over the house, making the garden glow, or the first rays of sunshine at dawn, as I stood with a little dish of porridge, the day breaking, the mountain waking. Or the touch of a sycamore branch on my face whenever I was feeling unloved and lonely. Nature kept speaking to me, in metaphors, in moments of connection with everything.

I began to investigate the offerings themselves. What was I doing? Who was I offering to? What did Tara represent? What happened at those steps that made my heart beat fast, and made me feel so connected to the fairy-like insects? What made me leave orchids or flowers for the black ravenous slugs that came to feed off the food? I began to care for slugs in the same way as I was caring for people. By looking after the slugs, I was also caring for myself: immersing myself in the practice, abandoning preconceptions, and allowing something else to arise as my fixation on the small self became weaker. I was mending my heart, and learning about love in a different way, with Tara as the facilitator.

I began to see Tara as a goddess, as an archetype of me, of myself as the goddess-woman who came out to play in the Maenllwyd kitchen. Tara's practice of active generosity and help was what I had come to the mountain for, not for the actual love of cooking. Through Tara, I invoked the wild woman in me, with her dormant, goddess heart. She came and danced in the kitchen, cooked, worked, sat and meditated. At first, the encounter with this part of myself was a complete surprise. It was a side of my personality that was sensual, free and playful; it was safe for it to come out in that sacred space.

This awakening led to creativity and artfulness. Whenever I felt connected to the wild of the mountain, I connected to the wild in me, and the magic in the kitchen roared, and could be tasted in the food.

One summer, I was cooking on a retreat with far too many men. The Guestmaster Fi and I were the only women participants. One of my favourite things on retreats is the presence of men. I like male company, love the charisma of male energy. I usually find it beautiful, safe, but on this particular retreat I was not comfortable, and I felt uneasy with the group's dynamics. There were several men who constantly whinged about not being given coffee: one participant spent the entire retreat waiting for me to make mistakes so he could "inform" the Guestmaster about "the cook's wrong-doings". The male energy was a strange one. I didn't like it, and the usual magic in the kitchen was not happening. Things got burnt, flavours did not develop to my satisfaction. I was really struggling with being there and I wanted to go home. Despite some delicious Thai orchids being offered to the slugs to feast on, despite the warm weather, this time they were nowhere to be seen. Tara seemed dormant too, as if her eyes were closed, mirroring how I felt, mirroring the fact that I felt deflated, low and uninspired.

Halfway through the retreat, Fi came to the kitchen for a chat. I told her I wasn't feeling at ease, that my inner goddess did not feel safe to come out to play. I said that I was unhappy with the food that I was serving, with the lack of inspiration I felt in the kitchen. She reassured me that everything was fine, but offered to come back later so that we could do a Tara awakening ceremony together. She told me to get a candle, some water, a piece of fruit, a flower and an incense stick. Whilst everybody else was meditating, we went outside and stood on the steps in the early afternoon with our offerings. She taught me the Tara mantra, *Om tāre tuttāre ture svāhā*. Mantra is a collection of words or sounds that act as a focal point for certain types of meditation, an aid to achieving spiritual transformation. Most Buddhist deities have their own particular mantra. Previously, Fi had shared her own experiences with Tara whilst practising as a Tenzo at the Maenllwyd. She reminded me that Tara represents compassion in action, and that I should ask her for help. I was a bit taken aback; did she mean asking aloud like in prayer? It felt weird. We knelt down, lit the candle and the incense, and offered the flowers and fruit. We also rang one of the rusty bells that hang from the beams in the house, which are usually used to summon the participants to the refectory for meals. We chanted the mantra until the words faded. Fi then guided me into asking Tara for help. I mumbled, felt self-conscious, but I truly wanted to shift the energy and I had not been able to do it alone. I asked for help, asked her about the lack of slugs - had the birds eaten them? We stood there, both talking to Tara, and the longer we stayed, the easier it became for me to open up to her. When we had finished talking, we each placed a hand on her knee and bowed. It was time to make the tea for the retreatants, and I went back to the kitchen.

What happened next was one of those moments which are difficult to describe: words detract from the depth and feeling of what actually happened. I suddenly felt that the kitchen was glowing and the Rayburn was roaring. People came and drank tea, munched on the cake, sat by the fire, went back to the Chan Hall. I joined everyone for the afternoon mantra, where we all chant the universal mantra, *Om*, in unison. When I returned to prepare dinner, the kitchen felt different. The light was purple, the kettles were jumping and spitting on top of the Rayburn, hoarily hot. The tiny space had suddenly become warm, active and inviting. I placed the supper ingredients on the wooden surface by the window, marvelling at how the sun made the vegetables shine. As I approached the windowsill to light the big, red candle that sits by the Buddha statue that I bring with me from home, I noticed a trail of slugs climbing up the window. It was as if they were trying to get in, to join me. A powerful compassion for the difficult participants arose in me; by dropping my concern with the energy of the group, I was once again allowing my practice to encompass everything, whether it was pleasant or unpleasant to me. I felt elated and grateful. The slugs must have returned to the steps because the following morning I could only see filaments of flowers left on the grass.

Chapter Six

Retreat Three: *Dancing with Death*

I was asked to cook a five-day Chan retreat at Bala Brook, a retreat centre on Dartmoor. I knew it would be a long drive, so I cut the journey in half and stayed overnight with my friends, Alec and Denise, in Gloucestershire.

The following morning, Alec wanted to take me to Stroud Farmers' Market. We wandered around and between stalls selling artisan cheese and rustic bread I spotted a woman selling cottage garden flowers from her farm. It was the best flower stall I have ever seen; it offered me a choice of all my favourites. I decided to buy some for the altar at Bala Brook, so I picked blue and burgundy cornflowers, delphiniums in several different shades, silvery-blue alliums and clumps of borage. Also, a little bunch of sweet peas wrapped in hessian.

I set off with my carload of food and flowers and, after collecting the organic produce I had ordered from the local farm shop, I left the main road and, accompanied by insect-chasing swallows, arrived at the house without getting lost. There is always so much to do when the cook arrives for a retreat: unloading, putting things away, gauging where the basic implements are and how they work. There are tables to set, preserves and condiments to sort out. On this retreat I also had to serve supper on the first night.

The house felt warm and embracing. The meditation room was light and airy, with polished wooden floors and lilac walls. As I explored, I found it was full of interesting artefacts: wall hangings, beautiful relics and Buddha statues. The kitchen was ample, with long, tiled worktops, large windows and plenty of light. A blue Aga surrounded by pretty majolica tiles splashed with scattered butterflies stood proud, the heart of this special new workspace.

I had heard that the house had no teapots to cater for large groups of people, so I brought three big ones with me. The Guestmaster said that a teapot is the English embodiment of *Kwan Yin*, the Chinese bodhisattva of compassion. I had to agree: a cup of tea warms the heart and offers comfort to people who are struggling with difficult issues on retreats.

I rummaged through the cupboards, looking for pretty serving dishes. It is important for me to serve meals in aesthetically pleasing crockery, and I found some in the pantry.

I baked a cake every day; I had to make do without scales, as there were none to be found. It was refreshing to experiment with cakes using my instincts. Cakes happened. I had only one mishap: an orange and walnut flapjack that didn't bind, and instead turned into a golden, delicious granola for the breakfast table. Nothing is lost in the Zen kitchen; even the food that we sometimes have to throw away is turned into compost which nurtures the ground.

We are not usually encouraged to write whilst on retreat, but this time I felt like it. With the luxury of electricity, I was able to scribble down a few notes before bedtime. I sketched out the basics of a dish I had created, made observations on my process, wrote a little poetry. Not speaking for days means that language does not flow easily: it is full of silences, gaps.

The house honours the small stream running alongside it with its name, Bala Brook. I couldn't quite see the stream from the kitchen window, but the sound of its flowing was a constant companion as I cooked. Knotted oak trees surround the banks, and granite boulders create some lovely pools as you walk up the garden.

Apparently the house's owner likes to take a dip in the pools. Although it was June, I was still wearing woolly socks and boots, so I was hesitant to follow his example, yet I felt tempted, called. I remember swimming outside in cold water as a child, fearless, beyond concern with cold or discomfort. I suddenly felt sad at the loss of that adventurous child spirit. As I grew up, I became fixated on what I thought of as comfortable. Since moving to this island, keeping warm has almost become an obsession; when I became a mother, I felt a powerful need to shelter myself and my children and keep us all safe. The girl that used to swim in cold mountain streams and jump into pools for the mere fun of it now spends her summers on an English beach, wrapped in blankets, merely looking at the sea, finding a book more tempting than swimming in the immensity of the ocean.

Yet I felt a yearning. I found myself thinking about bathing and flowing in the stream, screened by the gully of earth and ferns. I imagined the noise of my body in the water, the feel of my toes sinking in the mucky silt, my buttocks shrinking from the cold that stings the skin, then numbs it. I wanted to submerge myself, perhaps then loosing the grip of the frightened self in the steely moor water, like a river mermaid who had spent too long out of the water. I felt the flow of water resonating with the flow of the kitchen, of cooking. There was a sense of a freeing space to flow and float. Yet I remained standing by the pool, yearning rather than swimming.

I made leek, lemon and spring greens soup, a Nigel Slater recipe that had appeared in the paper the weekend before I came, and which I have adapted. It was vibrant, crunchy, tangy and full of heart.

The vegetables from the local farm were fresh and full of vigour. I opened each leaf of the lush spring greens to slice them, cherishing the texture and colour, taking my time. As I tore them off the stalk, they made a rubbery noise; they crunched as they came into contact with the knife. I sliced each leaf carefully, tenderly, looking and listening. I removed several caterpillars, taking them out into the garden with tender cupped hands, putting my heart and quiet attention into every second. When you look at something, even the humblest vegetable, with eyes of wonder, it is possible to witness the radiance of it, the "it" of a vegetable, a pulse, a grain.

Leek, lemon and spring greens soup

Serves 6

> 3 or 4 medium leeks
> 1 tbsp olive oil
> 2 carrots, chopped into small, bite-sized cubes
> 2 celery sticks, chopped into small, bite-sized cubes
> 1½ litres homemade vegetable stock
> 2 bunches of spring greens
> 1 lemon

Cut the leeks in half along their length, wash them and slice them thinly at a slant. Heat the oil in a pan, add the leeks along with some sea salt and black pepper. Lower the heat and cover them, so they can so they can sweat and cook but not caramelise. Don't overcook: always make sure that vegetables retain their colours.

Add the chopped carrot and celery, stir and cook for a few minutes, so that they seal. Add the stock, and simmer for five or ten minutes. Check seasoning. You can add a few squirts of tamari sauce as this enhances the natural flavour of the vegetables and adds body. Colour is key to this soup so don't add too much.

Wash the spring greens and cut each leaf along the stalk, following its natural line, then slice into medium strips.

Using a zester, remove the zest of the lemon and add it to the soup. Squeeze the juice of half of the lemon and put it to one side. Add the spring greens, and immediately remove the soup from the heat. Cover for a few minutes and check the seasoning. Stir in the lemon juice just before serving.

As the cook, I am often seen as someone who is not really taking part in the retreat. However, although I am not sitting all the time with everyone else, and I follow a slightly different schedule, it does not mean that I am not practising. In the silence of the kitchen I am on solitary retreat. I have learned to listen to silence, to relish it, marvelling as I first start to notice the noise of my mind, the voices in my head, echoing, murmuring. I am sometimes horrified by what I hear; the noise can be deafening and the thoughts disturbing.

Meditation is self-confrontation, and quieting one's mind is like obtaining a ticket to a forgotten yet familiar place, like walking towards an encounter with a long-lost loved one.

The path is often painful and on this particular retreat I was faced with a lot of sorrow. The question of death, of impermanence, kept arising. The recent and sudden loss of a dear friend that still felt raw, separation from my family in Argentina, a miscarriage in the early stages of pregnancy a long time ago: they all appeared like ghouls in my mind. Retreats are the perfect place to exorcise ghosts, yet on this retreat the ghosts were staying put. They wanted me to look at them, to give them attention. The rain that had not stopped for days made me feel as if I was walking around with the curtains shut. I was stuck on autopilot, performing my duties as cook, whilst trying very hard not to show that I felt as if I was falling apart. This, also, was part of the flow, part of the process and of the practice.

Bala Brook has no statue of Green Tara, as the Maenllwyd has, no steps to visit for solace, for a caress of a sycamore branch, or a glimpse of a gliding red kite above me. No black slugs feasting on orchids on the offering tray.

In this new place I was unsure what to do with the offerings. I had brought my little statue of White Tara so I made a small altar on the windowsill of the kitchen but it was not the same. So I made sure I spent time outside; I picked wild flowers for the tables and for the interview room. I made little posies of grasses and forget-me-nots, found dandelion flowers that winked yellowness. I turned to nature to heal my heart; I knew from past experience that it would speak if I was willing to listen, with nurturing sounds of silence, the un-semiotic undertone that connects with our spirit.

The Bala Brook kitchen had power, just like the one at the Maenllwyd. The active practice of cooking comforted me, helped me put self-concern to one side and concentrate on caring for others. There were no interruptions, just me and a line of bowls full of beautiful vegetables, mindfully chopped by the kitchen assistants during the work period. I was already cooking dinner when I realised that I had forgotten to buy tomatoes, so I had to improvise. A sweet potato tagine, which normally I cook with fresh tomatoes, instead featured copious amounts of a Turkish sweet red pepper paste, good ras-el-hanout spice mix, and fresh rose petals that I had picked in the afternoon and dried on the colander above the Aga. For the adventurous I put little bowls of harissa on the table with tiny teaspoons. Adding extra heat is always optional. It all worked out. It always does.

Sweet potato tagine

Serves 4

For the honeyed sweet potato:

> 500 g sweet potatoes, peeled and cut into slices 2.5 cm thick
> 50 g unsalted butter
> 4 tbsp honey
> ½ tsp salt

For the sauce:

> 2 tbsp extra virgin olive oil
> 1 onion, finely chopped
> 1 tsp coriander seeds, whole
> 1 tbsp tomato puree
> 400 g Italian chopped tinned tomatoes
> 100 g baby spinach leaves
> Coriander leaves to garnish
> Salt and black pepper

If, after slicing, you are not going to cook the potatoes straight away, place them in a bowl and cover them with water with a drop of lemon juice to ensure they do not discolour.

Pre-heat the oven to 220°C. Put the sweet potatoes in a roasting tin with the butter, honey and salt and place in the oven. Turn them over halfway through the cooking (after about 10 minutes) to colour evenly. Take care not to overcook: they should still hold their shape and have bite.

While the sweet potatoes are cooking, prepare the sauce. Heat the olive oil in a large frying pan and add the onion and coriander seeds. Fry until the onions are golden brown. Add the tomato puree, cook for a minute, still stirring, and then add the tomatoes. Continue cooking for about 5 minutes over a medium heat. Taste and season with salt and pepper.

Add the cooked sweet potatoes and all the juices from the pan to the sauce and stir.

Just before serving, stir the spinach into the tomato sauce and cook for another 5 minutes. Taste again and adjust the seasoning.

To serve, arrange the sweet potato slices and sauce and garnish with the coriander leaves.

The following night I made an aubergine dish with a parsley and tahini sauce, olive oil dripping off the serving plates: rich Moorish flavours. I like to alternate the simple with the opulent in the kitchen; in this way, people learn to taste the way other cultures taste, celebrating both abundance and frugality through shared meals. I made rich chocolate brownies with sea salt and rose petals; the petals sank into the batter as the brownies cooked, transferring their scent into the mixture.

Although I felt satisfied with the dishes I prepared, and with the general flow of the cooking, the deep longing remained. I struggled with low self-confidence and my mind remained agitated, as if on red alert. I had an interview with Jake, the teacher, who tried very hard to help me, to pull me out of this very dark space. I felt isolated and unconnected to the group; the issue of death kept creeping back. I realised that there were parts of my story lying dead inside of me: a love story that was cut dead before its time, which kept coming back to rankle me, uninvited; acts of betrayal by people I loved; aspects of my marriage that were so dormant they felt dead; the lost baby. I realised that I had never properly mourned the loss of that baby, opting instead for an optimistic view: I was blessed with two healthy children and I needed to get on with my life for their sake. What about my sake? Not confronting the death of something creates a morgue in your mind, and I was living with dead things inside my head, dragging me down, engulfing me.

There is a memorial stone by the wall at the side of the brook, with a bench beside it. It stopped raining, so I went to sit on it, taking my notebook and a cup of tea. The memorial bears the name of a young woman, perhaps the house owner's daughter, who, from the date on the stone, must have died in her late teens. Her memorial sits in a beautiful spot, by a tall oak whose dense branches twist around the trunk, entwined and racing against each other in search of light. I felt the loss of her, my heart felt bruised. It was as if I died a little. Her death, represented by the stone, reminded me of my own losses, my own little deaths, my own woundings. I knew that in order to heal I needed to revisit each wound again, remember what caused it, face it, give it recognition and confront the pain. An unhealed wound becomes gangrenous; it advances and rots whatever it has near. Like a mouldy peach in a fruit bowl: that same contagion of decay.

I was overcome by a sense of shame; I was alive, whilst the girl with her name on the stone was not. I felt hooked on my own melodrama.

The fast-running stream reminded me of loss, of tears I have shed, of home, but it also warned me: stop harking back, let the river run through you, let it wash your sores with its echoing sounds. Your life is now. Regain your foothold, go and serve dinner, take a walk, breathe deeper.

The sun was still out, though low in the sky, and everything glimmered. I set out for a late walk in my new aubergine rubber boots. Summer was buzzing, swallows flitted around my head, fat bumblebees copulated with hollyhocks. I heard dogs barking in the distance. A few black sheep were having their end of day social.

I walked uneasily up a rocky path, which I later discovered was a stream's course. I felt a strange sense of vulnerability, of the ground slipping underneath me. My rubber boots were pretty useless on this kind of terrain, but at least they were keeping my feet dry. I was sure I was on the wrong path. It all felt ominous. What if I fell and broke my neck? What if I died? More melodrama.

I climbed over the stone wall and walked along the next field until the bracken became too thick. Then I climbed back to the watercourse.

Up the hill, beyond the slippery rocks, I found a baby lamb's carcass. There was a deep beauty in its decay; the skull, teeth and woolly remnants lay flat on the damp soil. Its black trotters, so young and lustrous, were forever redundant.

The sweet smell of rot was pungently soothing: the earth nurtured by the banquet of the fallen. Maggots thrived and birds had pecked out its eyes, torn its flesh. This was the ancient glut of death out of which life flows again. It is like a dance, a primeval yet sacred dance, which never tires. It is balanced like a circle of beauty.

I stood, witnessing the compelling perfection of death, amongst all the thriving life around it. The carcass touched something deep within me, resonating with my anxiety around death.

You can't bring something back to life, but you can generate life out death.

But how do I do it? How do I deal with a carcass that inhabits my mind?

Do I leave it to simply take its course, until it disappears? The slow-rotting, pecking, maggot orgy would take decades.

Or do I shake it a bit, mulch it and turn it into a composting ground for something new to grow?

Suddenly the lamb's corpse exuded a dark splendour. I picked some ferns and flowers and made some posies, leaving them to adorn its shrine. I bowed, and continued walking.

Up on the moor, the sun filtered through the dark clouds, making a field of wild flowers sparkle. The green grass was luminescent. The wounds had become scars and I felt a sense of revival of my mood and spirit.

I was in the Dartmoor postcard and I was the postcard of Dartmoor at that particular moment. It was awesome and fleeting. I opened the gate into the field of flowers, threw off my wellies and felt the damp ground on the soles of my feet. It was a glorious and joyful moment of total presence.

I realised that all that mattered was now, being open to reality. For an instant, I understood that fundamental truth, with my whole heart. Everything else dropped away and my chest filled up with the glory of simply being alive. I stopped dwelling on death, and breathed just like the flowers around me. A feeling of newness, of beauty soaked me up; I felt like a pagan maiden.

I looked directly at the sun, and for a second, I shone with the dock flowers and buttercups, the red campions and grasses. Together we danced a secret midsummer dance with the wind.

Chapter Seven

La Granja

I grew up in a world of stories. Not only the gory fairy tales that fed my imagination, but the tales of the grown-ups around me, and the fascinating life stories of my family and the people we knew.

As soon as school ended we packed the car and went to spend the summer at my grandparents' house in La Granja. My dad commuted to work every day. The long three months of summer holidays were all about sunshine, playing, reading, social gatherings and family meals.

We loved to lie on the grassy banks outside the house, stargazing. The clear nights opened above us, a sky so vast it gave us a glimpse into the immensity of life, beyond all we knew and had read and imagined. All around us, as in a dance, the fireflies twinkled with the light of summer, like fairies who stored sunshine.

Hot and dry days made swimming our favourite pastime. We swam in the river and in the remote streams we reached after long riding expeditions. We also swam in friends' pools and in a small swimming pool in the grounds of the house.

The pool was built away from the house, at the bottom of the hill, away from the elms that encircled the buildings so that the sun could help the water lose its night chill. It had a funny shape and I was responsible for that. They built it when I was three and because at that time I was the only child of the family, they consulted me before digging the hole.

"What shape should it be?"

"I want it in the shape of an egg."

So, if you walk towards the hill, past the bakery and the chicken run, and keep going to where the pine trees are thriving and getting tall, you will find an odd egg-shaped pool with water as blue as the sky. Now I wish I had asked them to build it in the shape of a big castle or a giant hummingbird or the Leaning Tower of Pisa.

The pool was unfenced, and a long way from the house, so the adults were always worrying about us children swimming there on our own. For this reason they invented the story about the eagle.

The giant eagle lived in the rocks beyond the pool and we never saw her because she was always hunting to feed her greedy young. They told us that the eagle hunted for deer and hares and that if we were by the pool on our own she would not hesitate to turn us into prey. She would spot a stray child, fly low, grab it in her sharp claws and drop it not too far away, on the rocks at the top of the hill, break all its bones and then feed it to her babies. I think they made up the story because they were scared we would drown.

Like Lili's niece. She drowned when she was two. She used to play with my sister and then one day she tripped in the garden when no-one was watching, fell face first into a shallow bucket and drowned. My sister was too young to understand, but that summer she didn't want to swim anymore.

We all learned to swim when we were very little. My dad used to throw us into the middle of the pool and smile and shout: "Swim like little fishes!" He used to say that babies are born knowing how to swim. I think that my sister forgot out of shock.

Lili's niece had two older brothers. I used to play with the three of them, but after her death they didn't come to their grandma's house in the summer anymore. Lili's mother, Doña Maria, had come from Poland as a refugee from the war. She was a prisoner of the Germans and they put her and her family into a train carriage without food and water in the winter on a journey that would take days. She became ill and her tonsils were so inflamed and infected, she could hardly breathe. She told us that some of the German soldiers were compassionate enough to throw snow into the carriages as the people moaned with thirst when the train made its stops. She swallowed a snowball almost whole and with it, her tonsils. The snowball saved her life, otherwise she would probably have died of the infection.

She came to Argentina where she was reunited with her husband. They moved to La Granja, where they raised their two daughters. Many people who lived in the village arrived as refugees from the war; there was even a Bavarian-looking castle, hidden in the forest, built by the village philanthropist.

Doña Maria was an excellent cook. She used to fast during certain days in Lent and throughout the Easter weekend. On her fast days she used to cook, slaughter a pig, make cold meats and sausages, decorate egg shells and make the most delicious biscuits with poppy seeds. I was always happy when I visited her house. She kept animals and had a big kitchen garden. I loved digging potatoes with her; we unearthed our treasure from the mucky ground, removing fat earthworms and placing them back in the soil. She gave us a bucket and we would sit in the garden and scrub the potatoes clean with a brush. They looked like jewels.

My uncle, Jorge, who died suddenly when he was very young, was in love with Lili. He had a picture of her standing on the beach, tucked inside his book of Pablo Neruda's poetry, *Twenty Love Poems and a Song of Despair*. Jorge had a shark's skull with all its teeth intact. He would make up stories of wrestling with the shark to protect Lili while they were swimming in the Patagonian Sea. I used to touch the shark's teeth with the tips of my fingers.

Many Polish people used to visit Lili's mother, Doña Maria's, house. Sometimes a strange man would come and stay for the weekend. He would stay in one of the outbuildings. His face fascinated me. His name was Jorge, like my uncle, and he worked as a concierge in the city's smartest hotel.

He never looked happy; I always thought that he had suffered starvation during the war, as we would often see him eating old, dry bread. Lili recently told me that in Poland, before the war, he had belonged to an aristocratic family and was a renowned pianist. When the war broke out he managed to escape to Sweden with his wife and children, then to Switzerland and finally to Córdoba. I remember him making endless cups of tea from the same tea bag and dipping the old bread in it while he soaked up the sun.

On Easter Sunday we would go to Doña Maria's house for tea. In the dining room, in the centre of the house, she would set a long table, covered with a white linen cloth. On it, amidst small vases of cut flowers, she laid all her best china dishes, carefully filled with the food she had spent weeks preparing. There were ground almond cakes; different-shaped biscuits topped with icing, nutmeg or poppy seeds; smoked Polish sausages; homemade cheese; sweet pastries filled with quince jelly from the orchard and black bread with caraway seeds. She said that she loved to watch us eat all her hard work. She stood and smiled, her eyes watery. She would give us little chocolate eggs before we left, quietly, as if it was a secret. My mum said that she put all that effort into keeping alive the traditions of the family she left behind, so that she might feel a little closer to home.

Chapter Eight

Retreat Four: *The Art of Cooking*

It was a fine autumn, and I was preparing for the next retreat. Peter, who I had met on previous retreats, had requested to train as a cook, and we had selected a retreat led by John as the best opportunity to do the training. He flew in from Germany and came to stay for a couple of days in York beforehand. He wanted to get a sense of how I prepare. Preparing for retreats is like preparing for an expedition and he wanted all the details. I took him for lunch to my favourite Sardinian restaurant, before embarking on a foodie trail of town, looking for spices and ingredients in different shops, trying to get a sense of the food that called out to us. We chose Maldon smoked sea salt, pink mustard, and tiny chanterelle mushrooms from the Hairy Fig. We visited my local Indian shop and bought vegetables we had never cooked with before: kohlrabi, karela (bitter gourd), long string beans, mehti, baby aubergines. We filled baskets at Alligator, and bought a candle for the kitchen.

I wanted the ingredients to inspire him, rather than my teaching alone. I showed him the stock take from the previous retreat, and how to make lists based on this. This is important work, as it is better not to leave the house once you are on retreat. If you run out of something, you have to experiment with something else, use your imagination and trust that things will work out in the end. I taught him that all planning needs to take the environment of the retreat into account: who will be coming, and what the weather will be like. People eat less fruit in winter, but more cake. Women eat less cheese but use more toilet paper.

Peter had been a participant on my first retreat as a Tenzo. I remember noticing as his curiosity about cooking in the Maenllwyd intensified, just as the kitchen had intrigued me the first time I went there.

I also remember his kindness. When I first became a cook I thought I should follow as much of the retreat programme as possible, rather than concentrating on cooking wholeheartedly in the rudimentary kitchen. I didn't get enough rest and ended up developing debilitating migraines due to exhaustion.

It all became too much, but I continued cooking. Peter noticed, and volunteered to come and help me, instead of sitting; the teacher told him that his place was on the cushion. I was touched by his eagerness to help me, and for the rest of the retreat I tried to let him have a more hands-on role. I asked him to prepare a salad from scratch rather than drying up the dishes and putting them away.

We set off early and Peter was keen to know all the details, and scribbled down everything I said in a brand new notebook. I did find myself wondering if I was ready to teach him; could I really transmit what one does in the Zen kitchen? The dharma of the kitchen is rich and profound, but it is also personal, deep and silent.

Even the practical aspects of the kitchen didn't feel easy to communicate. Some cooks plan carefully, using Excel spreadsheets of recipes and quantities, but I have never been like that. Each retreat the menu changes, according to season, or the type of retreat. If a new type of grain is available in the local wholefood shop, I will include it at the last minute.

We both gasped when we started the drive up the track towards the house and shared a deep feeling of coming home, common to many who visit the Maenllwyd. Autumn here is glorious. It has an added splendour, as if the abundance of the season is palpable in the landscape, textured in the foliage of the trees, in the clusters of pine cones on the ground. Summer grasses and flowers linger on, decaying with grace. After we had unloaded the car and found places to sleep, I began the practical instructions. There was a lot to do. We started to unwrap the crockery from its coverings: the previous cook had not covered the crockery properly so we had to wash it all.

I showed Peter how we set the tables: each participant gets a plate, a bowl and a mug. A piece of kitchen towel is placed between the bowl and the mug. We found knives, forks and spoons, and the laminated prayer cards with the text for the grace on each side: one to recite before the meal; one to recite after. We put a card by each place.

We tidied the back kitchen, which was full of boxes of vegetables. We hung canvas bags from the wall to hold bread loaves and many other things we could not fit anywhere else. It looked like a huge amount of food, but we would be cooking for a big group. John was not very well. He had intense pain in his back, and was waiting for an operation. Fi was the Guestmaster.

The Rayburn was also in need of a lot of attention; she was playing up and was not as responsive as usual. The Rayburn is definitely a she, a sinuous enamelled woman with a warm heart, who is emotionally needy. You have to tweak her and talk to her and be attentive to her needs. She will only respond if you fully connect with her.

I remember one retreat during which I could not get her to heat up, no matter what I did: she was just not reaching the hot temperature needed to bake or roast. I tried all the troubleshooting suggestions in the cook's manual, without any success. After a couple of days, I went to talk to John. "I think it is you she wants. Have you been ignoring her? Can you go and kneel by her and see if you can persuade her to work properly for me?" He laughed and agreed to have a look. He came into the kitchen, opened both doors, had a poke at each corner to break the clinker loose (clinker is the hard cinders which get lodged on the sides of the burner pit and become solid). Kneeling in front of her, he touched her, gave her his time, but failed to distinguish anything technically wrong with her mechanism. Shortly after he left the kitchen she ignited and her attitude changed. She worked a treat from then on.

On this retreat, the thermometer on the oven door had stopped working, so we had no choice but to engage with her cycles of warmth and intense heat. From this tiny and temperamental oven we had to bake bread for lunch, two cakes a day, and cook supper. Knowing how and when to fiddle with the vents to get her hot, when to add coal, when to do the riddling, all became part of the flow. Rather than planning things in order, we had to act according to the way she was working. When she was hot, we baked the bread; when she was at a lower temperature, we baked the cake. The Rayburn is the perfect example of the kitchen's sensitivity and sensuality, and it was a challenge to share my understanding of her with Peter, whilst allowing him to learn for himself.

Peter kept his notebook to hand at all times, and scribbled notes as I showed him how or what to do. He told me he was not looking for the artistic details just yet; he just wanted to know the basic operations and the logistics.

I grinned at this. Artistic detail is not separate from the basic operation and logistics in the rudimentary Zen Kitchen. Art flows right into it and takes over as the only way possible to cook under such conditions. But I didn't want to tell him that. I was going to put all my efforts into showing him, silently, "doingly". I wanted him to notice. Lighting a flame underneath a wok full of golden olive oil and knowing the right moment to drop in the onions is not a science, nor is it empirical. It is an art of sensing with your heart.

The kitchen has three gas rings for cooking, two small ones and a substantial size ring on a stand which is ideal for the big wok. I never rely on the Rayburn's hot plate because the space is permanently taken by the three enormous kettles, which are kept full and hot at all times. The kitchen was designed by a tall cook, so shorter Tenzos often have to stand on a piece of railway sleeper to stir the food. The height of the rings taught me to work at heart level with the cooking; I learnt from a gut feeling rather than from instructions. Peter understood this pretty quickly when, as we started a soup base, notebook in hand, he was trying to count the lines on the gas knob to see what height of flame I was using to heat up the oil. I asked him to put his notebook away and stand by the heat, to get a sense of it. "You will know," I said. "And while you are doing that, without letting it become a thought or a preoccupation, be aware of the needs of the Rayburn. Don't forget that there is bread dough rising above it." If you lose yourself in an individual task, if you linger too long in a moment - and believe me, after a couple of days even onions frying in a bit of olive oil can make you feel like you are tripping - you will miss the flow of everything else. Peter came to gather precise data; he was also striving to learn how to do it perfectly, with no space for mistakes. In the Maenllwyd kitchen things go wrong, but everything always works out well in the end.

The first dishes we made together were courgette, lemon and coconut soup, and lemon cup cakes. The first batch of cakes burnt completely and went in the compost bucket. We started again.

We made the usual first day supper of mushroom stew and polenta with a green salad. Peter used batavia leaves, Turkish radishes, and toasted sunflower seeds. The dressing was delicious: we used cold-pressed sunflower oil, cider vinegar, pink mustard, a bit of honey and salt.

Peter followed me as I instructed the kitchen team. After the washing up was finished, we started with the food preparation. It is important for the team to wait for instructions before starting on a new task. That way I can show the helpers what shape the vegetables have to be chopped, as I try to imagine how I would like the soup to look, and which vegetable is to become the focus point.

Work periods in the kitchen are often frantic during the first half of each retreat, until people settle around the preparation tables and begin acquainting themselves with the way I show them to chop onions, with how to look at vegetables in order to connect with the way they would like to be chopped. The kitchen is a perfect place to practice mindfulness, awareness, a perfect place to practise Zen.

I remember one particular retreatant, a university student. He was a very keen Buddhist scholar. When he learned that he was to be part of the kitchen crew, he was mortified: he told me he was an intellectual and that kitchen work was too menial for him. I didn't respond. I have come across a lot of people who bow and follow the etiquette of flow and sitting and consideration to others in the Chan Hall, yet at the table they forget that they are practising, they forget that the table is also an altar, that practising Zen is not just for the cushion.

The intellectual practitioner worked half-heartedly in the first few work periods. I could sense that he felt that he was missing out on something by chopping onions, emptying teabags from teapots, or sweeping a floor.

Each work period I reserved a bowl of flat parsley and during the last fifteen minutes or so, I gave him the parsley, asking him to hold each leaf, break it off the stalk and tear it along the veins. I asked him to do it tenderly and told him that I was not in a hurry. For three days I gave him this job, and on the fourth day, instead of the parsley, I gave him something else to do. He looked disappointed. What about the parsley? Later, when the clappers announced the end of the work period, he asked if he could do his afternoon option in the kitchen instead of spending time in the library. He chose the kitchen as his option from then on and thanked me at the end for showing him that he could be meditative in the menial, that there was so much to be learned from a parsley leaf.

Peter and I were like two cooks in a cave, immersed in the practice. Alone in the house while the rest of the group was in the Chan Hall meditating or chanting, we cooked and prepared and cleaned. Before the retreat I was slightly apprehensive about sharing such a small space with another person but we managed not to bump into each other, getting into flow with everything else. I quickly became grateful for the teaching of teaching someone else.

John's pain got worse, so he took to staying in his room until breakfast. I offered to give him gentle back massages with essential oils: he accepted with gratitude. He was in a strange and beautiful space, in obvious pain, but he continued to give the most inspiring talks. Peter, Fi and I noticed how his teaching was changing. He talked about awe and wonder, about opening up, about reclaiming the child-like mind.

The skies were incredible, so full of stars it felt like it was about to fall on top of us. Fi and I sat on the bench outside the Chan Hall in silence and took it all in: the Milky Way and a few shooting stars.

We made minestrone soup using tiny fennel seeds and a lush savoy cabbage. We topped it with tons of fresh basil.

Quick minestrone

Serves 6

I often take my time when I make soups and I try to avoid using tins, but this recipe works really well for a hearty lunch. If you don't want to use chick peas, pearl barley works well, as do tiny shapes of pasta.

    2 medium onions
    2 medium carrots
    2 medium leeks
    5 stalks of celery
    ½ Savoy cabbage
    1 tbsp extra virgin olive oil
    2 cloves garlic, finely sliced
    1 tsp fennel seeds
    1 heaped tbsp chopped fresh rosemary
    2 400g tins of tomatoes
    1½ litres home-made vegetable stock
    3 good handfuls of fresh basil, torn
    1 400g tin of chickpeas
    Salt and freshly ground black pepper

Chop or slice all of the vegetables into bite-sized pieces.

Put the olive oil into a warmed, heavy-bottomed pan. First cook the onion until soft, then add the carrots, leeks, celery, garlic, fennel seeds and rosemary. Sweat over a medium heat until just tender (about 15 minutes).

Add the tomatoes and cook for 2 minutes. Add the stock, bring to the boil and simmer for 15 minutes.

Add the basil and the chickpeas. Simmer for a further 15 minutes. Add the cabbage, cover the pan and simmer for 10 minutes. Taste and season.

Fi was left in charge of leading the retreat while John was resting and I was moved by her approach to teaching. I had a beautiful interview with her in the hut, in which I described a moment by Tara in which I felt my heart expanding, spilling out through my inner contours and trickling down the steps. For a flicker of a moment, everything became my heart, until I rationalised it, went "wow", and in that second, the moment was gone.

By halfway through the retreat we were all pretty exhausted. The weather remained fine, but Peter and I never managed to find the time for a walk, let alone a rest. One afternoon, at tea, Fi and I were sitting on the bench outside for a few minutes, soaking up the sun, and Peter walked past us and asked, humbly, "Is it OK if I brush my teeth?" It was 4 in the afternoon. We smiled. He went to the stream and brushed his teeth and I could sense his tiredness, his back pain. We had many different coloured bunches of beetroot: orange, golden, stripy, and the conventional purple ones, so we decided to make beetroot cake. We followed a basic carrot cake recipe, swapping raw, grated carrots for the intensely purple, grated beetroot: we chose to use the conventional colour beets to make the cake. It was beautiful to see the juice colouring everything as we mixed the batter: the oil and eggs and sugar mixing with the beets like a magenta mess, like a kids' experiment. When we added the flour the colour softened. We thought we would be offering a pink cake, but as we sliced it, we discovered that it was green, grassy, unusual, and wholesome. It was definitely a cake for tasting the earth.

Beetroot cake

200 g wholemeal self-raising flour
2 tsp mixed spice
1 tsp baking soda
175 g dark brown soft sugar
2 large eggs
150 ml sunflower oil
Zest of an orange

200 g raw beetroots, peeled and coarsely grated
110 g sultanas or raisins
100 g pecan nuts

Pre-heat the oven to 200°C.

Grease and line a 10 inch cake tin.

First place the pecan nuts on a baking sheet and toast them lightly in the oven.

Whisk the sugar, eggs and oil together in a bowl with a hand whisk, making sure that the sugar dissolves well.

Now sift the flour, mixed spice and bicarbonate of soda into a separate bowl. Add the beetroot to the emulsion of sugar, eggs and oil, followed by all the remaining ingredients, apart from the pecan nuts. Mix well, and pour the mixture into the cake tin. Scatter the pecan nuts evenly on top of the cake. Reduce the oven temperature to 170°C and bake the cake on the centre shelf of the oven for about 40 minutes. It should have risen well, and be firm and spongy in the middle.

We also experimented with some of the Indian ingredients we had bought in the new Asian shop in York. Peter tweaked salads and made dressings and we discussed with John the theories behind a good porridge. We all agreed that the oats must be fresh and that you must add salt to the soaking water. We found this amusing: a German, an Argentinian and an Englishman in deep discussion about Scottish gruel. John was often in the house with us, which was a treat. He would sit in his chair, saying very little, but his presence was touching, frail and impermanent.

I took a short walk before tea on the fifth day, as I needed to let off steam and find my centre. I picked berries and brown bracken, which looked like milky chocolate. The mossy trees were dropping their leaves, getting ready for a lighter time. The skies were cloudless. Everything and nothing made sense. Two ravens flew high above me, their gargantuan beaks shining like liquorice sweets.

We made a lentil cottage pie topped with a root vegetable mash of organic parsnips, carrots, celeriac, suede, and butternut squash. We left it slightly lumpy, in case people wanted to decipher all the elements in what they were eating. We cooked the Puy lentils with onions, garlic, tiny cubes of carrot, cumin seeds slightly toasted, a bay leaf and lots of tamari sauce, which gave it a wonderful richness.

Braised lentils and lentil cottage pie

Lentils develop an earthy and rich flavour when cooked. Wholesome and perfect, the circular shape represents to me the infinite goodness of this humble legume. Before embarking on any lentil recipe, I like to toast them lightly in a pan. This enhances their smoky flavour and also allows you to spot any small gritty bits or broken lentils and discard them. After toasting, place the lentils in a colander or sieve and run cold water through them.

For braising, you will need whole lentils, so Puy or Castelluccio are best - you need them to be cooked through but retain their bite.

Serves 6

345 g Puy lentils
1 large onion, peeled and cut into long thin strips
1 carrot, peeled and cut into small chunks
3 stalks of celery, cut into small chunks
1 red chilli, some seeds kept, chopped small

3 small cloves of garlic, peeled and chopped small

A bunch of parsley

3 fresh bay leaves

A small bottle of Pilsner beer or a glass of white wine (optional)

⅓ cup tamari

2 tbsp extra virgin olive oil

½ tsp cumin seeds, whole

2 cloves

Very concentrated home-made vegetable stock

½ tsp smoked paprika

Sea salt and freshly milled black pepper

In a heavy-based pan big enough to hold two litres of liquid, heat the oil and add the cumin seeds, the cloves and onions. Cook them over a gentle heat until the onions are translucent. Add the garlic, carrots, celery and chilli, and allow to sweat under a lid.

Add the lentils, and mix well. Add the paprika and stir, then add the beer/wine and allow to evaporate. Add the tamari.

Add enough stock to completely cover the lentils and bring to the boil over a medium heat. Slow cooking is very important. If left over too high a heat, the gentle flavourings of all the elements will go into shock. Add the bay leaves and about half of the parsley.

Lower the heat and simmer until lentils are cooked but still retain a bite, approximately 30 minutes. Check the seasoning, adding sea salt and freshly milled black pepper. You might need to add more stock and tamari; be with the lentils and you will know how to tweak them.

See if you can find the whole cloves and remove them before serving. Add the remaining parsley. You can serve the lentils with rice, pearl barley, or on their own with a spoonful of Moorish aubergine dip (see p 143) or yogurt.

You can also turn them into a cottage pie. Simply make the lentils, omitting the cloves and smoked paprika, and add a few more cumin seeds and half a teaspoon of cumin powder.

For the topping you need a good root vegetable mash. I like to make this using organic root vegetables; the taste is sweetie-like and quite wonderful. Here I give you an idea, but feel free to use other roots: sweet potatoes, butternut squash, swede. Linda, who tested this recipe before the book was published, experimented with two layers, one of mashed parsnip, one of mashed sweet potato.

500 g carrots, peeled and cubed
500 g celeriac, peeled and cubed
500 g parsnips, peeled and cubed
500 g potatoes, peeled and cubed
50 g butter or the equivalent of extra virgin olive oil
Salt and ground black pepper

Place the vegetables in a large pan and cover with cold, salted water. Bring to the boil over a high heat, cover, reduce the heat and simmer for about 20 minutes, or until vegetables are tender.

Set the oven to 190°C.

Drain the vegetables. Return them to the pan, add the butter and let it melt into the vegetables, as you mash with a hand masher. You can leave some lumps, it adds texture and also intensifies the flavour. Season well.

Place the cooked lentils in an ovenproof dish, like a lasagne dish, and top them with the mash.

Cook in the middle of the oven for 20 minutes. Serve immediately.

It worked really well. I had used the leftover miso in the stock; this combined well with the spices, and the topping of mashed roots contrasted with the nutty lentils in quite a Zen way, as earth met sweetness.

People were collecting leaves and branches from their walks, and making arrangements around the house. It was if the landscape was inviting us to bring the outside in, and the house itself began to feel autumnal.

Peter began to notice the things that I have noticed over the years: the screeching noises; the kind spirits near the troll-like sycamore trees, between the house and the compost heap. Above all, he began to experience the magic of the kitchen, the alchemy of the process. Just as the vegetables and grains were transformed into food, so cooking had a profound transformational effect on the mind of the cook. The kitchen calmed our minds, just as a session on the meditation cushion allows things to arise, allows opposites to drop and gives space for the heart to take over.

On the last full day I suggested to Peter that we prepare an offering to Tara, as a celebration of the week we had had. I wanted to represent somehow the richness of the gifts we had received: the landscape, the kitchen, John's teachings, Fi's support and glowing presence.

I took an afternoon stroll up the hill. It was warm and sunny and I carried a basket with me. I was not sure what I was doing, but I collected things as I went up: pine cones, acorns, trippy mushrooms, different coloured leaves, conkers, red maple leaves, a fern that had already turned brown, berries, mossy bits of wood, tiny flowers still growing in the grass.

In the evening, after clearing up the kitchen, we were exhausted. We were beginning to doubt that we had enough energy left to make this offering, but we knew we had to continue.

We had decided to make a mandala. Mandalas are a representation of the universe, they depict both the microcosm (in our case, our work in the kitchen) and the macrocosm (the world around us). We asked John for advice on how to design one and he mentioned one traditional Tibetan form: the five circles. These circles are called Excellencies and they represent the teacher, the message, the audience, the time and the location. This made sense to me, as I had been making natural circles on Tara's steps for years, using flowers, things I found on my walks, and other kitchen produce.

Mandalas also demonstrate impermanence. Tibetan monks spend days creating mandalas from sand, only to sweep them away as soon as they are finished. John's visible vulnerability and the rapid deterioration in his health made the mandala particularly poignant: all was changing. Anxiety about the future hung over us.

We worked on the mandala, so tired we were hardly able to murmur a word. We made little piles of the earth's fruits: the red hawthorn berries; the tiny Indian cucumbers; handfuls of red lentils; leaves from all the trees around us; long red chillies. Tiny mushrooms and orchids were left in the kitchen, surplus to requirements. Acorns with missing tops, green and brown ferns, cinnamon sticks: all were to take their place. We had not used the *karela*, the bitter gourd from the Asian supermarket, so it too became part of the offering.

We realised that is was going to take us hours and it was too late to stop. We refrained from saying anything, but I knew that we both regretted having started it. Our backs and feet and legs ached. Peter took a break, stretched his back and did some exercises on the floor. The creation of the mandala felt like a pilgrimage, charged with a solemn heart and physical pain and soreness. By the time it was finished, we knew why hadn't stopped and why we had to do it. It was beautiful, like life dancing through the richness of nature.

The following morning was the last of the retreat. After breakfast we all gathered to offer the mandala to Tara. John sat on the bench leading the chants whilst Peter and I carried the offering towards the statue. We offered the tray with humility, stinging backs and tears in our eyes. We chanted the Tara mantra until all our voices faded; the only sound remaining was birdsong. *Om tāre tuttāre ture svāhā.*

The retreat ended, and we left behind the offering to Tara just as it was. It was a symbol of our sweat and tears, of what we had learned, all left to be eaten by wildlife, to be shifted by the wind, to be soaked by rain.

Chapter Nine

Porridge

I have never been a big fan of stodgy food. Growing up in a warm climate made me accustomed to light, Mediterranean-style meals: continental breakfast, a big lunch, afternoon tea and then late night supper. They were high protein, low carbohydrate meals, full of fruit and vegetables.

It amazed me how much I changed after just two winters in Britain. My body needed more calories, more fuel. Butter became alluring. Rich food, which had never appealed to me, gradually became a necessity. I developed a sweet tooth, falling in love with chocolate. On more than one occasion I even succumbed to crumpets, those bizarre gooey buns that cannot be chewed unless they are dripping with fat.

Still, I could never eat porridge. I even found it difficult to look at. I remember my husband's stories of when he used be a professional fisherman on the Isle of Wight. Porridge played a major role in his fishing tales: he claimed that it gave him the sustenance to endure the arduous days of dredging for oysters. He told me how he used to soak cracked oats with salt and coconut overnight and eat two big bowls of porridge before setting off in Bee, his boat, before dawn. He said that porridge kept him full for longer than any other breakfast. For him, it is the perfect breakfast, full of goodness and comfort. For me, it used to be a meal I would only eat as a last resort, an "eat to survive if there is no other choice" type of food.

I did not know this when I first went there, but porridge is a key part of the Maenllwyd breakfast tradition. The cook brings a big pot into the dining area and after grace the teacher fills each retreatant's bowl using a big, bronze ladle. On the first morning of my first retreat, as I sat silently not knowing what to expect, a bowl of hot porridge appeared in front of me. There was no escape. The first bite was unbearable. I didn't know what to do. I felt it would have been rude not to eat it. I was eager to test myself but I felt like crying. With great relief, I spotted a pretty dish full of stewed fruit: lightly spiced apricots, pears and prunes. I added some to my bowl. The second bite was still difficult, so I added a spoonful of honey. The third bite made me fear that I could not face a fourth. There was a little dish containing a brown grainy powder, which I sprinkled on what was left of my nightmare. It was *gomasio*, ground toasted sesame seeds with toasted sea salt. This made the fourth bite much better: nutty, salty. I remember the porridge ripping out whatever warmth I felt inside; it sank like a rock in my stomach. This was no comfort food for me. I didn't even manage to finish the porridge. From then on I opted out, gripping my bowl firmly to myself as the server approached.

When I first became a Tenzo I resented making porridge and I never ate it. I felt like Babette, making a foreign gruel for the people she cared for, nourishing them but not herself. Her nourishment came from the care she put into making it for them. I loved cooking everything else but found serving porridge very uninspiring.

Then, one winter's day at the Maenllwyd, I was rushing to get breakfast ready. I was alone in the house, dawn was breaking and a twinkle of golden light was filtering through the front window, into the dim kitchen. If I strained my ears, I could hear the chanting from the Chan Hall across the yard. I had retrieved the cold milk from the stream, and I was decanting it into earthen jugs, getting everything ready for breakfast. I suddenly realised that I had forgotten to check the porridge.

As I stirred it vigorously I looked closely at it, trying to connect with the pot and with what was inside it. The oats had swelled and merged into one. Surely this food was as beautiful as any other food I cooked, but I still found it bleak, dull, almost sad. It puzzled me. This was good, honest food - why couldn't I like it?

Then a vivid image came to me. It was a picture of a graveyard covered in snow. I was standing on a wood block, with a wooden spoon, unlocking my memories, stirring something other than porridge. The image of the graveyard reminded me of a story I had once read. It was the opening chapter of my great-grandfather James's biography, written by my grandpa Alec, which I had read as a young teenager. It starts with a sentence describing an intensely cold afternoon in the cemetery at Kilbirnie, Scotland, in 1876. A small group of people gather around an open grave, listening to a Presbyterian priest give a sermon, paying respects to the deceased. The dead woman is a young mother called Agnes. Everyone is thinking about her distraught widower, John, and the three small children left in his care. The confused and bereft John, still numb from the blow of losing his wife, stays behind by the grave after everyone leaves, not noticing the snow falling around him. He ignores his friends' pleas to go home and only returns very late at night to his miner's cottage, where he falls ill with pneumonia and dies four days later.

So, my great-grandfather James Clifford lost both his parents at the age of four. His sister Agnes was six, the little one, John, one. Granny Knox, although frail and old, took the three orphans on and looked after them until she died. They were extremely poor. The book tells how she made their clothes out of worn-out adult garments, so raggedy that they could not even attend church sometimes. The children spent most of the year barefoot. Their nutrition was basic and humble: they ate only porridge and potatoes.

James was an outstanding, well-behaved student who excelled at school. When he was seven, his teacher, the severe Mr. Fulton, suggested that he might be able to get a university scholarship. Yet his poverty meant that he had to start work in the coalmine at the age of twelve. I was twelve myself when I first read the story, and I remember my horror when I read that at my age he worked twelve to fourteen hours a day and only saw daylight on Sundays. Even today, it feels grim to think of this remarkable man's childhood. How many times had I read that first chapter, which told how he worked hard at the mine so that he could complete school at night, how he became a missionary and ended up in Argentina, the land of plenty, where the sun shines every day and where nobody eats porridge.

Suddenly my breakfast-making reveries revealed why I felt the way I did towards porridge: my sadness at eating it, the association of eating porridge with a child's devastating loss and grief, with poverty, with cold feet. In stirring that porridge I also acknowledged the magic of the kitchen. I was coming into relationship with my ancestral stories, which are so much a part of who I am today. If I could understand the emotions still alive in a story of my past, projected into a bowl of food, how many more stories were there to unlock?

How many more ghosts of my past were waiting to come out and reveal their sorrows?

Nowadays I cook porridge lovingly on retreats, always with a dedication to my Scottish ancestors. Porridge was what gave them strength and made them survivors. I make it with equal parts of organic jumbo oats and porridge oats, which I lightly toast and leave to soak overnight in a 1-2 ratio of oats to water. Often I drop a cinnamon stick into the porridge, which gives it a wonderful fragrance once it starts to heat up.

I cook it in the morning for about an hour, adding a good pinch of salt, stirring it every time I pass the pot whilst I am getting breakfast ready: lining up bowls of stewed fruit; separating the vegetables for the morning's work period; going back and forth to the stream to pick up the cold milk and Tara's tray; slicing bread.

It took me a while to learn how to get the right consistency. I almost beat it to make it creamier, as this helps the oats to release their starch. Even today, I have to be in the mood for eating it, and it has to have a salty element in it, a bit of runny honey, and something else to add texture.

That breakfast, my first ever at the Maenllwyd, was my first encounter with gomasio: little wooden bowls full of a brown textured powder that smelled nutty. I don't recommend it for every meal as sesame has a strong taste and I prefer good quality sea salt for seasoning dishes, but gomasio awakens curiosity and it is often what makes people break the silence on retreat, to ask me what it is. So I must include it amongst my recipes.

It originates from the macrobiotic tradition, the Japanese philosophy on whose principles I often draw in my cooking practice. Macrobiotics esteems sesame seeds as a virtuous ingredient. When mixed with salt and toasted, the seeds acquire a natural healing quality. Sesame is believed to hold the key to a healthy digestion and helps reduce sodium levels (although it contains salt, the difference is in toasting it). It is rich in minerals and a good source of both protein and fibre.

You can make gomasio at home. Don't make too much, as the seeds tend to go rancid after a while. Small portions will last a long time, as you only need a little. All you have to do is grind together dry-roasted sesame seeds with roasted sea salt.

For the grinding, ideally you should use a *suribachi*, a Japanese mortar that is used with a pestle called a *surikogi*. This mortar has serrated edges, which makes the grinding easier. However, this is by no means essential and you can use an ordinary pestle and mortar or an electric grinder.

Gomasio

¼ cup raw, unhulled sesame seeds (I prefer brown or yellow)
1 tsp table salt

Place seeds in a clean, dry, frying pan and toast on low heat, stirring often, until golden or until they are just starting to pop. Try to take them off the heat before the popping takes place. Use the lowest setting on your hob. It often takes 20 minutes; the potency of the taste is in the toasting. It will also make them easier to grind later.

Place the toasted sesame seeds in a bowl and allow to cool.

Roast the salt in the same pan, again on the lowest setting on your hob, for about 10 minutes, until it shines.

Mix the seeds with the salt in the mortar, and grind. Be careful not to grind it into a powder, as the texture of the seeds is important.

The first thing I do after I unpack the car is make fruit compote. I make enough so that it lasts for two or three breakfasts. As with all my cooking on retreat, the quantity and variety of the fruit changes. In summer months I add black plums. In the autumn and winter, when people tend to eat less fresh fruit, I use apples and pears. I slice bananas, and experiment. This is a basic recipe, but you can make it your own, according to season.

Dried fruit compote

200 g unsulphured apricots
200 g pitted prunes
100 g raisins or sultanas
200 ml freshly squeezed orange juice
2 tbsp honey
1 cinnamon stick
2 cloves
2 cardamom pods

Place all the ingredients in a heavy-based pan and add enough cold water to cover all the fruit. Leave to soak for a couple of hours. Add another half litre of cold water and bring to the boil. Reduce the heat and simmer for 30-40 minutes, or until the fruit has softened and the liquid is syrupy and thick. Allow it to cool down and serve at room temperature.

Chapter Ten
Retreat Five: *Cooking in a New Kitchen*

It was time to cook yet another autumn retreat, but this time there was a difference. The Maenllwyd had been modernised over the summer, and I knew that the kitchen would be different.

I came a day early to get the place into a nice flow. I found a new Rayburn and a new range cooker, along with new shelves and work surfaces, and freshly painted white walls. The boxes of organic vegetables slotted perfectly onto the new shelves. I had a bunch of ornamental, cabbage-like flowers for the altar and freesias for the kitchen window and for the slugs. John admired the freesias so I placed a long stem on the altar in the refectory so that he could smell their scent when he blew out the candles after each meal.

Early morning: the kitchen sizzled and the sleepy new Rayburn toasted a tray of sesame seeds, slowly, at a snooze pace. The first stages of what was to become a bitey, courgette soup sweated away on top of the new range cooker, which now stood by the window where the counter space used to be. It was a misty start to a beautiful autumn day; the valley was clouded over by what looked like a bowl of different coloured ice-creams, that creamy pastel subtlety of pistachio, raspberry, peach, hazelnut. The sunlight filtered through the mist, showing off the landscape's deliciousness.

This was to be a *Hua-Tou* retreat. A Hua-Tou is a "critical phrase", an open-ended question designed to concentrate all thoughts upon a single point. A Hua-Tou makes you look profoundly into the nature of simply being. It is not a question that requires an answer. One has to allow it to repeat over and over, locking it into the mind so that it arises continuously, whatever activity one is engaged in, like brushing your teeth or peeling an onion. The idea is to allow the Hua-Tou to take over one's whole consciousness, even when you are asleep.

I began working on mine as soon as the retreat started. It was "What is it?" or "What is this?" What is it? I started to use it, to bring practice into the focus of whatever it was that I was doing.

There is a lovage plant in the kitchen garden. Although it was close to packing up for winter, I was delighted to find some new tender leaves for the first night stew. The leaves become tough and bitter by late summer, but on the last retreat I had given it a good pruning, to encourage new growth. I tied the branches with string and dried them over the Rayburn and stored the dried leaves in jars for the winter months.

Lovage is in fashion again and I am glad. This old English herb is pure summer in your mouth.

I was first introduced to lovage around the time I came on my first retreat. I was running a country market in York and met Rachel who cooked with us for a while. We became friends and shared many culinary secrets. I remember hippy afternoons in The Menageries, playing in the woods, building bonfires, and eating hearty food picked from the huge kitchen garden. We made herby salads with cold-pressed sunflower oil dressing, and lovage was a key ingredient. I fell in love the first time I tasted it.

Lovage is from the celery family and it has a unique flavour. People often say it is a mix between parsley and celery, but I think that lovage tastes only like lovage. I associate it with love and abundance, with ancient herb gardens, and with potions and playfulness.

This parsley of love makes fantastic summer cordials, and can substitute for parsley in a lovage sauce which works beautifully with roast or boiled potatoes, nut roasts and steamed vegetables.

Lovage sauce

425 ml milk
3 cups chopped fresh lovage (I prefer just tearing it with my hands)
20 g plain flour
40 g butter
Nutmeg
Salt and freshly milled black pepper

Put the butter into a saucepan and heat until the butter has melted.

Gently add the flour and using a metal whisk start to mix the flour and butter almost immediately. This is a stage where speed is important, as you want to avoid the flour getting lumpy. Keep whisking.

When the flour has absorbed the butter and the mixture is smooth and homogeneous, begin adding the milk, a little at a time, continuing to stir the mixture. Use a wooden spoon this time, rather than a whisk. Each time you add some milk, wait for the sauce to come to a boil and for the sauce to thicken. The result should be a creamy and smooth white sauce with a firm texture. Season with salt, pepper and freshly grated nutmeg, and add the fresh, chopped lovage to the sauce and stir well. Adjust seasoning and serve.

Fresh lovage cordial

Makes a small bottle.

> 50 g fresh lovage
> 300 g sugar (any type is fine)
> 300 ml boiling water

Put the lovage leaves in a bowl, cover them with the sugar and begin pounding with a pestle to crush it all into a paste. Cover with the boiling water, stir well, cover and allow to infuse for a few hours, ideally until the liquid has cooled completely.

Sieve into a saucepan, squashing and pressing the lovage to extract as much flavour as possible.

Heat the pan over a moderate heat, stirring until the sugar has dissolved completely. Bring to the boil and allow it to boil for at least three minutes.

Pour into a warm sterilised bottle and seal. Leave it to cool before chilling. Shake before use and consume within one month.

Lovage works really well with mushrooms, especially wild, or mixed button and Portobello. I tend to make a stew of mushrooms and lovage on the first night of a retreat for supper, because it is relatively simple to prepare. Also, it is so meaty and rich that it comforts all the fearful carnivores who dread a week without their chops. The stew can also be turned into a mushroom and lovage pot pie by adding a sheet of flaky pastry and blasting it in a hot oven.

Mushroom and lovage stew

Serves 4

> 1 large punnet button mushrooms
> 4-6 large field or Portobello mushrooms, cleaned and cut into thick slices
> ⅓ cup tamari sauce
> Extra virgin olive oil
> 2 medium onions, chopped
> 2 celery stalks, chopped
> 3 carrots, chopped
> 4 garlic cloves
> 1 tbsp mirin
> Fresh or dried lovage

Heat the olive oil in a wok or frying pan and sauté all the mushrooms in small batches, as this allows them to cook better. When they are cooked and softened, place them in a bowl until you have cooked them all. Mushrooms love oil so you might find that you have to keep adding oil while cooking.

Heat one tablespoon of olive oil in a casserole dish and fry the onions until soft and translucent. Add the carrots and celery and allow them to sweat. After a few minutes, add the mushrooms, then the garlic. Stir for a minute and add the tamari and the mirin.

If you want your stew to be very liquid, you might want to add some vegetable stock.

Allow the stew to cook for another twenty minutes and then let it rest so that the flavours seep into each other and the juices become inky. Check seasoning. Add the lovage just before serving.

I usually serve it with polenta. I grew up eating polenta and I must admit I was never crazy about it. I didn't like the texture or the blandness. In Argentina it is cheap and by no means as glamorous as it has become in the UK. The Italian settlers brought it with them at the end of the eighteenth century. The journey of maize had come full circle, returning in a different form from how it was used before the Europeans came to the new continent. For the Italians, it was their staple, their *piatto unico*, representative of the drudgery of the feudal land they had left behind. We tended to eat it at home at the end of the month, when we got to the back end of the pantry cupboard, and of the bank account.

Only my grandmother Fina's polenta could tempt me: her meaty, slow-cooked tomato sauce, tons of butter and *queso fresco* topped the polenta. She told me how, in the farm where she grew up, they cooked *polenta blanca* in a three-legged cauldron in the yard, over embers. They stirred it with a thick, wooden stick which they held with two hands. The cooked polenta was then turned upside down onto a giant wooden board with a handle. They cut it into portions with a piece of string. Any leftovers either turned into toast, or were left to dry in the sun over a metal disc and made into biscuits. Now I love it, and I tend to make it on retreat. As I pour the polenta into the boiling water, first stirring with a whisk to avoid lumps and then heartily with a wooden spoon, I remember earlier times and different eras. The stirring not only brings out the sunshine of its colour, but also that bit of Italian peasant immigrant in me, as I cook in a tiny kitchen in the Welsh mountains, with my grandmother whispering me directions: "Add more salt, it's too thin. What do you mean, no butter?"

After the work period I sat on the bench to think about what I had in the pantry and scribbled down possible dishes, and which vegetables from the boxes I brought to use for soup. I tend to alternate dishes I know work well and I can make with my eyes closed, with more experimental meals, in which I test a new ingredient, or put together something completely new. New dishes tend to be more time consuming.

In the old kitchen, having only the Rayburn's tiny oven meant that I had to plan carefully for what needed baking and roasting throughout the day, as it takes a solid fuel cooker a long time to reach the desired temperature. Perhaps the new range cooker would allow me to be more spontaneous and adventurous, but I was still mourning the old layout.

I found it hard to remember what the pantry had looked like before the facelift; it was so light and functional now, ideal for working in the afternoon. The south-facing window felt more open, the whole space felt brighter. However, the new Rayburn was leaking fumes and I could not warm it up enough to bake. The fire pit was glowing yet the oven temperature would not exceed 150 degrees. But everything else was flowing beautifully: the lamps providing light with their hissing noise; open cookery books; chopping blocks; balsamic vinegar in bottles; compost buckets filling up twice a day and the same old kitchen smell.

For lunch the next day, I decided to make celeriac and parsnip soup. Celeriac is a relative of celery. What you eat is the root, which has rugged skin and root ends like hairy tails, which tuck in together at the base. It tastes a little like celery but it is nutty and sweet and has a wonderful fragrance. You can eat it raw in salads but I prefer it cooked, especially in autumn and winter soups. I soaked the peeled chunks in acidulated water (cold water with either lemon juice or vinegar). If you want to boil celeriac it cooks in 20 minutes. Roasting it will take 35-40. It makes a great gratin, and combines with other root vegetables to make a delicious mash.

Whilst lunch was being served, I took a tray to Tara and as I kneeled before her, a beautiful butterfly landed on my arm and tangled its legs on my woolly sweater. I started to notice the gifts of nature. What are they?

The weather kept inviting me to walk, so I followed the stream up the steep path, unhurriedly caressing the gentle old trees on the ledge half way up the hill. The sound of the water reminded me of Sally, a member of the WCF, who had died the previous year. Her ashes were scattered close to the stream by her family and friends. Sally had become part of the landscape and I reflected on the fact that we are always part of the landscape, never separate from it. Each breath I took reminded me that I was alive, as were the rocks and the bracken, the crows and the trees on the ledge.

The previous night I had left a bowl of organic chickpeas soaking in cold water, so that today I could make harira. Harira makes me think of souks and Moroccan markets. There is something magical about markets. I can think of nothing better than walking around stalls full of produce, pulsating with the energy of the earth. I treasure the banter with the stallholder and the proximity to the ingredients. Shopping in markets is truly interactive: you can be offered suggestions; you can feel, taste and smell before buying. My senses awaken with the displays. Colour, contrast, quality and human contact are what make shopping at markets my most sensual way of buying food. Wherever I travel, it is the markets I first look for, where I get lost and touch and taste, and where I interact with locals.

One of my most memorable food journeys was a trip with friends to Morocco a couple of years ago. We took the car ferry from Spain and our first stop was a beautiful town by the sea called Asilah. In the morning, after a sociable breakfast of fresh mint tea, fresh orange juice, toast with olive oil and fresh, curdy goat's cheese, we wandered around the market. It was my first visit to Morocco and I was fascinated by everything. The simplicity and perfection of the ingredients; the herb stalls; the women selling little blocks of musk; the bundles of artichoke stalks to be used in tagines; the rugged oranges with stalks and leaves; fresh strawberries, olives and dates; snails in slimy baskets; the intensity of smells; the vibrancy of the place; the aliveness.

Once we were inside the market, we each decided to stroll around in different directions and I came across a small man with the wrinkliest face. He was wearing a wool *djellaba* with a pointy *qob*, or hood. The weather was still cold and everyone was wearing heavy robes. I even saw a man using his *qob* as a shopping bag, carrying bread and vegetables inside it. The little man with the wrinkly face looked like a medieval monk and was pushing a granny's trolley with a big stainless steel soup pot inside it. I stood next to him and watched as he interacted with two men who wanted to buy what was in his pot. He made some small paper cones and then opened the lid of the pot to fill the cones with warm, freshly-boiled, giant chickpeas. They looked so beautiful. I was not hungry, but very curious. He sensed my interest and handed me one with his spoon. How simple and tender, how wholesome and nutty, how perfect was that chickpea. I allowed it to melt slowly in my mouth. I have always known that food does not need to be fancy to be delicious, and in that moment the whole universe opened up in my mouth, as I tasted that simple example of its perfection.

Harira is a spicy chickpea soup from Morocco, and my recipes always vary, depending on what I have. Because it is rich, I like the fact that I can always improvise.

Every time I make it I think of that chickpea from Asilah and I return to that market. I have to plan ahead as cooking the chickpeas from scratch makes such a difference: tinned chickpeas are sweet and clammy in comparison. Sometimes I use little cubes of preserved lemons as their salty sharpness adds a punch which is a subtle yet noticeable top note as you taste the soup.

Harira

Harira always tastes better the day after; if you allow time for the flavours to develop, you will achieve a more substantial and richer taste. As I write this, I am staying with my friends Ceci and Victor in Tarifa, in southern Spain. The Moroccan women who work in Victor's restaurant are currently fasting for Ramadan and they make harira. It never tastes the same twice. Some days it has lentils, or more vegetables, or coriander. It works wonders with broad beans. You have to tweak it to get the flavour you like.

You can always make it spicier by adding some harissa. I would not suggest adding it to the soup, but I normally serve harira with little dishes of harissa for people who like their food spicy.

Serves 4

2 tbsp extra virgin olive oil, plus extra for serving
1 onion, chopped into small cubes
3 garlic cloves, finely sliced
1 stick celery, chopped
2 carrots, chopped
1 tsp fresh ginger, grated
2 tsp ground cumin
1 cinnamon stick
200 g chickpeas (dry weight), soaked overnight

A generous pinch of saffron strands, soaked in ¼ cup of boiling water
A preserved lemon cut in small cubes (optional)
1 dark vegetable stock cube
1 pinch cayenne
400g tomatoes, deseeded and roughly chopped
Half a large bunch of coriander, chopped
Half a large bunch of parsley, chopped
1 red chilli, deseeded and finely chopped
Sea salt and freshly ground black pepper
Juice of half a lemon
2½ litres cold water

Soak the dried chickpeas overnight in plenty of cold water.

Heat the olive oil in a large saucepan and fry the onion until browned. Add the garlic, chilli, celery, carrot, ginger, cinnamon and cumin and fry for another minute.

Add the drained chickpeas, saffron and tomatoes. Crumble in the stock cube and heat until the mixture is bubbling gently, stirring to dissolve the stock cube. This should take about 5 minutes.

Now add the preserved lemon and the water. Bring to the boil and leave on a gentle heat to cook for over an hour, checking that the chickpeas are cooking and softening.

When you feel that the chickpeas are cooked, add half the coriander, the parsley, cayenne and salt and pepper. After five minutes or so, check the seasoning. You might need to add a little sugar to reduce the acidity of the tomatoes. Stir for a minute.

Add some lemon juice and check the taste. Remove from heat and leave to cool for a few minutes before serving. You can't really taste food if it is too hot. Just before serving, drizzle with extra virgin olive oil, and add the rest of the coriander.

The retreat continued: the flow of the kitchen was different, and just as I had anticipated, having a gas cooker meant that I didn't have to rely on the temperamental Rayburn to bake in, but the "new" Rayburn was behaving worse than the previous incumbent. I mourned the loss of the relationship I had developed with the old Rayburn. The biggest loss was the hard wood counter under the window. It was a sacred space, like an altar for preparation, where the light of the afternoon filtered perfectly as I prepared supper, enhancing colours, enlivening sometimes dull looking concoctions. It was here that alchemy occurred in unexplained circumstances. But I had to drop this attachment and find a way to work with the new arrangement. In the old setting there was a real sense of abandonment of self. In order for me to become one with the kitchen, the intuitive cook inside me had to come forward. Now cooking was more straightforward, but still full of challenges.

I found that I had more time to join in the Chan Hall, and above all I was not as tired. Perhaps the new kitchen was helping me to find more space, but I kept resisting it. This space felt unnecessary. Or was it that the modernisation of the kitchen had made the practice of cooking less challenging?

I reflected on this to John, at interview. He thought I was exaggerating, but I felt sure that I needed to push myself in a different way. I wanted a challenge from him. He annoyed me by suggesting that I change the menu. I came out of the interview fuming. I bashed the pots whilst I cooked lunch; my mind was raging. "Do something else, train in something else, you could do so much better than this. How dare he? I do not plan menus!" And yet, after I served lunch and saw everyone tucking in, I was able to see that I was doing what I was supposed to be doing.

So far I was managing a walk a day. Every day, I made a mandala offering with things that I found on my walks. One day I made a beautiful circular offering with leaves, acorns, and some death cap mushrooms. Someone had picked the mushrooms on a walk and then left them for me on the kitchen counter as an offering, thinking that they were edible. I didn't like the look of them and remembered Pam's advice never to trust mushrooms people pick for the kitchen. She had said, "Put them on display but never touch them." I kept looking at them and feeling my stomach crunch. I asked for a second opinion later: they were indeed death caps. Fortunately, I followed the teachings and my instincts, and did not put them in the stew!

I told John that I had seen a fairy. He knew exactly what I meant without having to explain. He got excited, and asked, "Where? Where?" Fairies are insects that I come across in moments when I am still and open. They are merely bugs, flying insects that I have never seen before, but somehow, when I see them, in my own perception I have gone beyond classifying them as an insect. I undress them of the word that defines them, and at that moment I begin to perceive an otherness, an intelligence, the simple magic of life. They are so beautiful, so aware and so utterly perfect. Tara always gives me these tiny moments, when I go to retrieve or offer the little dishes. I get nudged, caressed, touched by nature and life in ways that are overwhelming. I awaken to notice beauty in things to which I had used to pay no attention.

Today at lunchtime what caught me were the insects: the broken-winged fairy, which struggled to climb up Tara's leg; a tiny yellow spider constructing a web, perhaps in preparation for the broken-winged bug; two ladybirds whose colour I had never seen before standing on Tara's head. This is "it", those moments are it, diving into "it", being present with the bugs, my self being completely overtaken by their presence.

What is this?

Another day and such beauty around me: sitting by Tara on the steps in the warm sun. The stream was flowing merrily down the hill, chilling the milk bottles.

The purple potato side dish from the previous night's curry had turned into a colourful Spanish omelette with a bit of an Indian flair. I had never before used purple potatoes, but I would do so again, as I found the colours fascinating to work with and the texture waxy. People's faces were full of wonder, asking the question "what is it?" as they prodded the spuds with their forks, trying to decipher what they were.

The four people in the kitchen team were full of generosity and awareness. After the work period, John came down for his third coffee of the day and sat on the bench next to Dan, enjoying the sunshine. They were a pleasure to watch: a truly dashing brace of men.

I had left some onions cooking with cumin seeds and salt. Onions are the foundation of my cooking and I like to pick the big Spanish ones as time is limited: peeling and chopping one of them yields the equivalent of three or four small ones. I like to cook onions well, until they are translucent. It is important not to hurry them, not to burn them. Burnt onions turn bitter. I cover them and let them sweat, as steam helps in the cooking. I love stirring them and watching as they change from the uniform yellowish colour to crystal-like translucent strips that sweat and ooze. They seem to be asking to be joined by others: vegetables, spices, stock. Slow cooking makes such a difference to both flavour and digestion.

I used the onions as a base to make the lentil cottage pie base, and I made the topping with vegetables grown at Evan's farm, down in the valley: parsnips, carrots, celeriac, butternut squash and potatoes. The mash was so rooty and sweet, and the bits I left chunky added a wonderful texture.

What do I come here for? Why do I feel like I wanted John to change my task? I come here to cook, and if cooking is what I came for then it is what I do. I cook, I soak quinoa, I burn aubergines on the stove until they char, I taste, I sieve, I boil and steam and squeeze and chop, crush and slice and stir. I measure and I bake, I trust, invent, improvise, I create, experiment, dance, fail, start again. I run, set tables, arrange fruit bowls, wash up, always aided by the constant soundtrack of the roars, the clangs, the drips, the hisses and rustles and rumbles of everything around me.

As I opened the refectory door to ring the bell, to tell people that the food was ready, a red kite flew quite low, over the sycamores and across the Chan Hall's roof and started circling around the hut. The numbers of red kites have increased with the years and they seem to feel less unnerved by human presence than they used to.

What is this?

Why do I keep coming back here to the Maenllwyd, to cook, to break my back, to get exhausted, to peel away my layers of suffering, to stir the

109

big pot of emotions? I arrive with a carload of raw materials, like the artist walking up a hill with a blank canvas and a bag of paint and brushes. When I reach the house I cannot help myself from smiling. Whatever anxiety I have brought with me drops. As soon as I go through the last gate my body shivers, as if I am arriving somewhere strangely familiar, like the sacred garden of my childhood. Arriving in this remote corner of Wales, the house and particularly the kitchen has always felt like coming home. It was many retreats after the first that I realised that I was coming home to myself. In some way, all the elements, particularly silence, meditation and cooking were enabling my true self to come out to play.

Some evenings, during supper, John would break the silence with an instruction and a question.

"Hold your question! Where is your mind? Hold your method!"

On this particular evening he said, "Where else could you get a meal like this?"

After supper, people sat by the fire. There was a beautiful full moon. The nights were cold but the days were full of autumnal glory. It was now Thursday and the week had almost gone by. I finished the day with a wonderful walk all the way up the hill. The colours of the landscape were whimsical, as the season started turning. As I came back to the house, I came across the group of sheep that had been moved in the evening so that they could graze behind the house. An old raggedy sheep and I had an eye-to-eye encounter. Our gazes locked; it felt like an attempt at communication.

What is this?

The beauty of life pulsating, the perfection of a single brown lentil on the palm of one's hand, the complexity of my biochemistry, the billions of years of evolution that are my hands. Moss growing on a bench, alive and thriving. Being a witness did not feel enough, yet I immersed myself in its lushness. I gleamed and it filled my heart. My heart, like a beautiful chunk of moss.

The last day was a Friday. I made apple cake with cranberries, cinnamon, pecans and rose petals. It was a wholesome bake, and was completely invented. There was no recipe, so there would never again be one like it. At John's request I made cauliflower curry with spiced rice, a raita of yogurt with cucumber and fresh mint, and chapattis. I had a lot of oranges left so I cut them into wedges and sprinkled them with cinnamon. This is another Moroccan discovery. The oranges need to be sweet and juicy and the sprinkling of cinnamon light. The combination is mind-blowing. Nothing but fresh oranges and cinnamon.

The kitchen was slowly emptying, things were going back into boxes, crates and pantry bins. It was a sad feeling yet I was ready to go home. On the last evening, John prepared a beautiful evening puja in the Chan Hall with a lot of chanting and playing of Tibetan instruments. The altar had never looked so glorious. As the cabbage flowers dropped their leaves, they had become little cradles for conkers and balls of moss.

Chapter Eleven

Fina

When I was little, my grandmother Fina's house in the village of La Granja was always busy. It housed a big general store, a bakery and a post office. Life pulsated in every corner and the village's daytime social life revolved around their big fridge counters where tapas and aperitifs were served to friends and shoppers just before lunchtime. My uncle Jorge lived with my grandparents. He loved walking in the wild terrain around La Granja, and was forever finding orphan animals on his early morning walks. He used to bring them back to be domesticated. So apart from dogs, horses and chickens, we also had the friendliest wild pigs, baby deer, and wild cats that looked like mini leopards and had to be kept in a cage.

My grandfather and uncles used to get up very early to bake bread for the shop, and then deliver it to houses in the neighbouring villages. People left a shopping bag hanging from a tree or a hedge outside their house with a note saying how much and what kind of bread they would like for the day. They paid at the end of the month: everyone had credit. If I was able to get up early enough, I would accompany my uncle on a delivery in the new Citroën wagon or in the *estanciera*, packed with giant wicker baskets filled with French bread, croissants and *criollitos*. Criollitos are a square, flaky, bread bun made with a lot of fat, so they melt in your mouth. Deliveries were very sociable and at the end of the round, if I was lucky, we would stop at my Great Aunt Marta's house. She was my grandmother's youngest sister. She loved to cook and had enormous fig trees outside the cottage-like house. Much of the garden was wild, like a meadow. She had an orchard and a kitchen garden where she grew beautiful vegetables. Her breath always smelled of garlic. She used to make and sell *alfajores*, which are buttery biscuits sandwiched with dulce de leche, a thick caramel which we use in most of our cakes and sweets in Argentina. I was not allowed dulce de leche because of my dairy allergies but she loved to indulge me, so she always sneaked one to me as I hid under the table where my uncle couldn't see me. Even today I ask people to bring alfajores when they are visiting from Argentina.

Work was hard and food was important. My grandfather, Oscar, who was of French Basque descent, expected cooked lunches and suppers. Fina made big dishes of ravioli and of perfectly shaped gnocchi. She slow-cooked rich stews and ragus for hours, baked polenta and roasted her own chickens in the bakery's wood-fired oven.

She was always thinking ahead, often rising at dawn to begin her preparations. She used to take me to the peach trees and show me which ones to pick for her favourite dish of baked peaches. I loved being lifted to pick the peaches, prodding them with my finger to check if they were ripe enough. I stroked the furry surface and inhaled the honey peach scent. We would put them in a wicker basket, wash them and halve them and line them up on a baking tray with a sprinkle of sugar and sometimes a few sprigs of lavender. We would do the same with figs, pears, plums and quinces.

At the end of the summer, Fina and my mother would make jams outdoors, in a giant copper pot over embers. They stewed the fruit slowly, with sugar, sometimes leaving it to reduce for a couple of days. My job was to decant the jam into a pretty dish and prepare the tray for afternoon tea in the garden.

Their cellar was full of treasures. My grandfather kept a store of cured hams and salamis from Colonia Caroya and let them hang from the oak beams. The shelves were packed with jars, wine bottles and junk. People came from the whole district to buy food in the shop because the quality was so high.

Occasionally we used to go to Colonia Caroya, which was one of the first agricultural colonies created during the Italian immigration of the nineteenth century. Groups of settlers from Friuli were allocated farms in these fertile lands. Fina's family came with very little, escaping the feudal farming system of their homeland. They left their country and families to build a new life and never looked back, as it was impossible for them to return home, even for a visit. They worked hard, building up their lives from nothing, including each brick and tile of the house. They made mattresses from wool and the women made all the clothes.

The things that I used to take for granted take on a new dimension now that I live in a different climate. I miss the hot afternoons, sitting eating pears with Fina. I miss the way she quartered and cored the pears and the way we shared them: the slurpiness and the joy. With sun-bleached tea-towels on our laps to soak up the pear juice, we sat in the shade and talked, sharing stories, planning supper. We prepared big trays of peeled pears to be blasted in the wood-fired oven, sprinkled with a little brown sugar, butter and a splash of La Negrita rum. We waited by the oven while the pears baked. If I listened carefully, I could hear the noises of the heat softening the fruit, caramelising the seeping syrup like treacle. To accompany the baked pears, we made crème anglaise from scratch, using eggs from her plump hens. I still remember the intense yellow of the custard.

Last year I took Fina to her ancestral home in Colonia Caroya and spent the afternoon with her cousin Pablo who now lives in the house. There were grapes on the vines, and a well-kept vegetable garden. A crowd of pears sat ripening on a wooden table. I kept looking at them and finally, just as we were standing up to walk around the grounds, I asked Pablo if I could have a pear. The moment I bit into it, all the pear memory in my body began spinning. I tasted that pear, and with it, I savoured my childhood once again.

Alfajores

Makes approximately 40 biscuits

260 g cornflour

170 g plain flour (good quality OOO flour is even better)

2 tsp baking powder

½ tsp baking soda

200 g butter

110 g caster sugar

The yolks of three eggs

1 tsp brandy or cognac

Zest of one lemon

Dulce de leche

Desiccated coconut

Dulce de leche is a thick, milk-based, caramel sauce. You can buy it in many supermarkets and in specialist shops. You can try making your own by boiling a tin of sweetened condensed milk for an hour or longer; the thicker the consistency the better. Leaving the tin unopened, place in a pan full of water and boil for an hour and ten minutes, making sure that there is always plenty of water for the tin to be covered while it boils.

Sift together the plain flour, cornflour, baking soda and baking powder and set aside.

Beat the butter with the sugar until creamy and the sugar has dissolved.

Add the yolks to the butter/sugar mixture one by one, mixing well after each one.

Perfume with the cognac and the lemon zest.

With a spatula incorporate the dry ingredients, mixing well. Bring the mixture together into a firm dough.

Leave the dough to rest wrapped in cling film in the fridge at least for an hour. You can also freeze it for up to three months.

Pre-heat the oven to 160°C.

Roll the dough to a thickness of 4-5 mm. If the dough is too crumbly to roll out, bind with a little milk. Cut into round discs, about 4cm across.

Place the discs on a greased oven tray and return to the fridge for five minutes.

Bake the biscuits until they are firm but not brown.

After cooling, you can either store the biscuits in a tin or make the alfajores the same day.

Sandwich the biscuits together with a thick layer of dulce de leche. Roll the sides of the sandwiched biscuits in the coconut, pressing slightly so that the coconut sticks to the dulce de leche.

Alfajores will keep in a cool place for up to seven days.

Chapter Twelve
Retreat Six: *The Pilgrim Cook*

She walks in beauty like the night
Of cloudless climes and starry skies.

~ George Byron

This was my third retreat in less than a month: a *koan* retreat led by Simon Child. A koan retreat is an investigative retreat in which practitioners take on a traditional short pithy Zen story (a koan) to practise with. The stories are sometimes seen as puzzles to work your way through, but this may be a poor understanding. The koan is a story that often relates an encounter between a master and disciple, usually in ancient China, and the koan often has an implied question, which is usually "what is going on here?". There is no answer to a koan and those that pick them up looking for an answer will struggle long and hard. The koan is really a sounding board: what is important is what resonance it generates in you and what responses it eventually pulls out of you. You start off puzzling about what happened a thousand years ago, but the true response is about what is happening here and now in you.

The weather had been cold for the first two retreats, and the landscape was barren after the harshest winter in my memory. At times I wore three layers of clothes to keep warm. On this third retreat, despite the heavy snowfalls and two digit sub-zero temperatures of not so long before, things were beginning to revive. As I got ready for the retreat I noticed that bulbs were coming through. The tender maroon shoots of what would become our lovage plant were sprouting: their see-through, green leaves looked like flowers. Birds sang raucously, matching my excitement with theirs. Things were waking up, the sun was shining, and we had made it through the winter!

I felt serene and tranquil after a very emotional couple of weeks. I could not help marvelling at how much can be achieved with a raw, open, Buddha heart. The intensity of the practice had left me in quite a cathartic space, and I was working on old issues with a different understanding. I felt an enormous compassion towards my own suffering and towards my family, who are so affected by it.

I made a leek and potato soup thinking of my son, Ian. I miss my children when I come on retreats, but they are not keen on the type of food I cook here, mostly because I like experimenting and they prefer familiar flavours, for which their dad is a reliable source. Ian loves leek and potato soup, and I was missing him a lot.

I melted some butter in the pan and added a squirt of olive oil, a pinch of sea salt, freshly milled black pepper and a few saffron strands that rapidly began to seep their yellow-redness into the fat. I had never done this before, but I knew that saffron and potatoes were a good combination so it was worth an experiment. I only had a few leeks so I started with onions, cooking them until translucent, then a chopped carrot and a few stalks of celery, cut to the same size as the carrot. I added the carrot and celery to provide flavour, rather than to be noticed much. Then I added the leeks, a bit more seasoning, and covered the pot. I turned the flame to very low, and left the vegetables to cook and sweat. Then I added new potatoes, skins still on, sliced roughly. I don't liquidise soups: a chunky leek and potato soup is highly comforting. I strained the homemade vegetable stock onto the soup and let it cook slowly for an hour. Then I let it sit until half an hour before serving, checked the seasoning, and brought it back to the boil.

I had an interview with Simon. I felt washed out emotionally, almost as if the recent Japanese tsunami had had an effect on my soul. I reflected on our attachment to comfort, to the idea of life as a permanent thing. Yet in a second, everything can change. Life as we know it can be devastated, flattened, washed away. And despite it all, life goes on. The earth keeps moving and people go about their business.

I baked two trays of flapjack. It was like toffee when it finally cooled down, different, with a gooey, yet crunchy, texture.

For supper, I picked a few of the new leaves of lovage, just for a hint in the stew. I had dried some in the Rayburn last autumn, but the intensity of the new plant took the mushrooms to a different dimension.

The next day was beautiful, but cold. I had a burn on my leg from the hot water bottle I had taken to bed with me the previous night. It had blistered and looked nasty. I made pot after pot of green tea for the tables at meal times, to keep people warm. Chinese green tea leaves benefit from being re-used, so I kept recycling them.

In the afternoon, I made brownies. Baking always feels like an adventure. I topped the batter with dry rose petals I had brought back from Morocco, which made the two trays look beautiful as they went in the oven. The petals were hardly noticeable after the brownies cooked, but there was a hint of rose in their flavour. If people really tasted each bite, they noticed.

Scented brownies

350 g good quality dark chocolate (60%+ cocoa solids)
250 g butter
3 large eggs
250 g dark muscovado or brown sugar
80 g wholemeal self-raising flour
A drop of good quality vanilla essence
A handful of rose petals

Pre-heat the oven to 160°C.

Grease and line a shallow 9 inch square cake tin

Break the chocolate into pieces and cut the butter into chunks. Place them in a bowl over boiling water to melt. Allow to cool.

Whisk the eggs, giving them plenty of air, until they are fluffy. Slowly add the sugar, until you get a shiny and well-blended mixture. Add the vanilla and gently fold in the cooled, melted, chocolate mixture.

Sift in the flour and mix carefully, making sure the flour blends well with the batter.

Pour into the tin and bake for 30 minutes.

Don't panic about the softness of the cake, it will harden as it cools down.

Allow to cool before cutting.

You can add toasted nuts to the brownie mixture before baking (toast them lightly in the oven as it is heating up, but keep an eye on them so they don't burn). I sometimes sprinkle some Maldon sea salt on top of the mixture, just before I put it in the oven. Sea salt and chocolate is one of my favourite combinations. You could also try sprinkling the brownies (again before they go into the oven) with dried rose petals from the garden or from a wholefood shop (commercial roses have high levels of pesticides).

The colour of the valley was shifting from green to brown in the afternoon light. I sat with my tea on the bench and focussed on a foliage-free silhouette of two trees intertwined, connected through their growing branches which were wrapped around each other, like one tree with two separate roots. The bareness of the tree was a flawless depiction of the end of winter.

The sycamores were budding fatly, ready to explode into leaf. I had been thinking of training as an analyst; if I did so, I would have to give up coming here to cook. Sitting in front of this spectacle filled me with sadness as I wondered if I would return.

I love the rusticality of the Maenllwyd, the woody, crackly, drafty spaces, the dust, the rugs, the pictures, the ancient boots above the mantelpiece and the spirits. Above all, I love the sycamores and the kitchen with all its magic of ancient druidic energy, the slugs by Tara that connect me to my inner goddess. Everything reminds me of my nature, and helps me regain it.

I had a strong sense that the muse was back. I felt creative, connected to the landscape around me. Simon had lent me a super lens for my new camera. I experimented with black and white photographs, but it was colour that won out, colour that became more and more intense as the retreat progressed.

The green tea leaves swelled inside pots, were re-used, recycled to the last. One, two, three, four times they infused, hot water extracting taste and goodness.

The house settled during the rest period after supper. People were hovering around, drawn to the squares of leftover brownie and halva on a pretty plate on the coffee table by the fire. There were only ten of us. Someone had fallen asleep and was snoring. The assistant Guestmaster Doug stared into the flames and glowed like a mirror of fire.

The pears were not ripening, so I moved them to the shelf above the Rayburn.

I started to memorise my koan:

A monk once asked a pilgrim:

"What is your style of practice?"

The wayfarer replied:

"I wrap my sandals in my robe."

"What does that mean?" asked the monk.

"I go down the mountain barefoot,"

Answered the pilgrim.

Cooking was a joy on this retreat, the spirits of the kitchen and my own heart working together in harmony, spontaneously creating. The carrot cake had some added ingredients: fresh pineapple cubes, coconut flakes, and walnuts. I marvelled at the process, at the alchemy of transforming ingredients into food. Some of the flavours were sublime, but it felt like I had little to do with it. I was simply channelling creative energy; it felt like I was just one added element in the process, rather than the creator. I was simply allowing the food to express itself.

The kitchen brings me back to something ancient that inhabits me, a non-linguistic space, hard to explain in words. It is something innate, inherited, alive in me, in each cell, in the complexity of data that we are. The knowledge that allows me to mix the cake batter, the way I sense temperature or concoct a soup: these are not skills learned at school but a deep understanding of food that comes from within and from the ingredients, from the tools, the fire of the stove. The sycamores help, as guardians, nesting my muses the slugs, and murmuring together. The sounds of the stream; the walls, cracks and draughts; a sheep skull reminding me of the fleetingness of life: all are part of the kitchen team, they join in the effort. The Maenllwyd kitchen is a place of potions and pain, of joy, of taste: the barefoot cook is alone with a job to do, her sandals wrapped in her apron.

I took a walk up the hill to stand by the lonesome tree at the top of the track. On my way back I removed my boots and socks. It was painful, but I got a strong sense of each step I took, feeling each grain of sand, each thorny stick, coming into contact with the soles of my feet. I denied myself comfort in order to feel, and I noticed the humility of taking each step, as my bare feet became brown and dusty. I felt alive as I washed my feet in the stream and dried them with my scarf.

The following day was implausible, almost summer-like, so unusual in the Welsh mountains. It felt like a precious gift; surely we would have to pay for it at some point. It had a tint of prophecy, surely foretelling a ghastly summer ahead. I had lived on this island long enough to be cynical about the weather. Just in case I was right, and because here, better than anywhere else, I inhabit the present, I tried to soak up copious amounts of sunshine. Later I took a blanket and sat by the stream and re-read my cook's report. It amused me to see how almost everything I describe on retreats is repetitive: the trees, the birds, the steps, the valleys, the insects, Tara. Yet two experiences are never the same. Nature teaches me new lessons each time, using the same teachers.

As I sat scooping pomegranate seeds on Tara's stony steps, red, juice-drenched fingers and sun-rays filling a steel bowl on my lap, I lifted my head. I caught a glimpse of a man as he washed in the stream, half-hidden by grasses. His chest was bare, his skin was pale and his eyes flickered, lupine, as he splashed his torso and washed, crying out and sluicing his pain with mountain tears. Like a wolf that howls his aloneness, the entrenched solitude of his nature, that depth of sound with no noise resonated in my heart as his kept beating.

Tara felt very active and the spirits and animals kept coming to feed off the offering tray. That morning I had made a circle of "out of date" pumpkin seeds surrounded by pink hyacinth flowers, with a rusty bell in the middle. By the afternoon only the flowers lay scattered around the steps; the bell lay behind a group of daffodils. There was a sense of troll activity, of force.

"Teacher, show me the way."

"Have you had porridge this morning?"

"Yes."

"Then wash your bowl."

I had some spare time as I was waiting for something to cook so I started to clean and scrub the kitchen, dragging the metal bins outside so that I could sort out their contents. The back kitchen pantry began to sparkle.

I made Chinese black rice and rye grain bake, with crunchy stir-fried vegetables, handfuls of tamari-roasted almonds, feta cheese, slow roasted tomatoes and fresh herbs. I kept the grains al dente, as this increases their nutty taste, and means that they won't overcook when they go in the oven with everything else.

I started to prepare purple kale, slicing the dried end off the stalks. The leaves were beautiful. I got the wok very hot, added some water, tossed in the kale and some salt and put the lid on. After a few minutes I removed the kale leaves with metal tongs and arranged them on platters. I scattered some toasted seeds on the top; it tasted of simplicity and perfection.

Despite the small numbers, people were very generous and volunteered to help with the evening washing up. For the first time in ages I decided to take the compost bucket to the heap. I was usually too tired by this stage and my back had had its fair deal of lifting, but something was calling me to do it. It was a beautiful, strangely warm, starry night; I had put a bowl full of tea lights by Tara, and the space glowed. I walked up the hill carrying the bucket, the head-torch beaming light and showing me the way. As I approached the large wooden box I sensed a presence, and as I got closer I noticed a big beast feeding of the pile of food waste: a badger. Rather than running away, it jumped at me, frightened. I dropped the bucket and remained still. We stood there, staring at each other, until the badger ran away, towards a hole on the metal wire in the fence. I smiled. I had never seen a badger in the flesh before, only the unfortunate dead ones by the side of the road. I bowed to the furry garden troll and returned to the kitchen to make some tea.

The lunchtime soup the following day was a celebration of winter vegetables. I made a leek base, sweating away leeks in a bit of butter, salt and pepper for twenty-five minutes. Small cubes of celeriac were sealed in the wok using olive oil. Once the celeriac was cooked and golden, I added it to the leek base, together with some salt and tamari sauce and then filled the pan with the usual homemade vegetable stock.

In a heavy frying pan, I heated olive oil and fried half a handful of grated ginger, and in the meantime I toasted eight or nine pecan nuts and a tablespoon of coriander seeds. I allowed the ginger to almost caramelise and when the seeds and nuts were golden I put them together in a pestle and mortar and crushed them slightly. I added them to the pan with the oily ginger and mixed them well. I added the spicy ginger nut crunch just before serving the soup. It tasted wonderful: tiny explosions of heat, sweetness and nuttiness, like a dervish dance of flavour in my mouth.

For afternoon tea, I made little fairy cakes with lemon and Madagascar vanilla butter cream icing. Someone said they were chirpy little cakes. I got help setting the table outside, which I covered with a blue and white check tablecloth. It was lovely to be part of a group of retreatants having tea with Tara on the lawn in early March.

The pilgrim cook and her practice. In her practice she has learned that there is no aim, nothing to attain, just that beauty of walking the path: in the sunshine; in the snow; in the red, fallen leaves of autumn and in the muddy puddles. Walking with nowhere to go leaves room to notice where are you walking, what is on the ground, what the landscape has to offer. There is nothing to attain, just porridge to be cooked, a pot to be washed, bread to be made, the offerings to be offered. The cook's heart, her spirit and her body are present at all times. Her feet are bare.

If only things always felt so straightforward. That night I hardly slept, I felt run-down and overtired. The effect of three retreats in a row was taking its toll, and I woke up with a blinding migraine. I had no tablets and I needed some. I told Simon that I was going to try and get everything ready for lunch and go into town, to the chemist. The Rayburn had been quite temperamental and there had hardly been any hot water for washing up. Just before I left I had words with the Rayburn. I explained that I really could do with a hot bath, that it would be kind if she had some hot water ready for my return.

At around ten in the morning I had everything ready: cake, bread rolls, soup and all the supper prepped, ready to be cooked later. I drove to the next village and went straight into the chemist, with no time to spare. Driving down and back up the track took its usual half an hour, because of all the gates, so I didn't linger. The Rayburn was literally roaring when I got back. I bowed to her, feeling that perhaps she understood. I made a quick cup of peppermint tea and prepared a bath. I eased myself into the bath, relieving my aches and pains. I got out of the bath, dried myself, dressed, collected my things and had a short rest. The tablet was working but migraines tend to leave me debilitated, shaky and exhausted. I had so much to do and I felt I needed a good day's sleep, but I could not. I felt weepy. I wrapped up, wiped away the tears and went outside to kneel in front of Tara with a stick of incense and a hyacinth flower. I asked her to heal me and help me get through the day. It was probably the first time I had prayed so desperately.

By the end of the day I felt better.

I sat on a blanket on the lawn by John's room and gazed at the deep blue sky beyond the bare branches. The organizational marathon of this morning had paid off and I managed to lie horizontally for a good hour. What a wonderful place this was, what a gift it was to be here. I saw a tree that had not even dropped last year's dead leaves yet. Didn't it know it was spring? Trees know what we struggle to grasp, just by being, growing and losing their leaves. Their pilgrimage is upwards and outwards.

I realised that I had been seeking to "get" somewhere, and I had been there all along. I had been seeking something to unlock me, and by seeking I was losing focus. By seeking love I had placed love outside of myself. If I stopped seeking, perhaps I could find the calm and serenity that gives way to opening.

I pickled mushrooms, put them in sterilised jars and made labels. I would sell them at the end of the retreat for the bursary fund, which helps people with low incomes to attend retreats. I roasted peppers and put them in jars with a bay leaf, a garlic clove, a few peppercorns and extra virgin olive oil. I also made some raw carrot pickles with fresh lovage and whole spices: "the barefoot pickle collection."

I had a good interview with Simon and told him about my conversation with John on the previous retreat, when he had dared to suggest that I "change the menu". I suddenly realised that John's response was a direct challenge to my ego. What a wonderful way of teaching me. On that same retreat I truly began to write; before I used to be too tired to write anything apart from simple notes of dishes I invented. There used to be no time to write, and now there was. John wanted me to write. Tenzo practice was teaching me, nurturing me, connecting me to myself. So much has been cooked already, so much remains raw.

We had afternoon tea in the garden again. I made a cappuccino cake, which was lush. The coffee lovers relished every bite.

Cappuccino cake

I make this cake in a big tray and cut it in squares. It is rich and moreish.

> 250 g butter, softened
> 280 g wholemeal self-raising flour
> 250 g golden caster sugar
> ½ tsp baking powder
> 4 eggs
> 150 ml natural yoghurt
> 1 tsp vanilla extract
> 1 tbsp cocoa powder
> 100 ml strong coffee, cooled

For the icing:
> 140 g icing sugar, sieved
> 225 g mascarpone or cream cheese
> 1 tsp vanilla extract
> Cocoa powder for dusting

Pre-heat the oven to 180°C. Grease a 20 x 30 cm baking or roasting tin and line with baking parchment.

Beat together the butter, flour, sugar, baking powder, eggs, yogurt, vanilla, cocoa and half the coffee in a large bowl with a whisk. Make sure there are no lumps left. Transfer into the tin, and then bake for 25-30 minutes until golden and risen and a skewer poked in comes out clean.

Allow the cake to cool in the tin while you stir the icing sugar into the mascarpone. Add the remaining coffee and the vanilla extract, and mix well until smooth. Spread over the cooled cake. Using a sieve, dust cocoa powder over the iced cake.

I joined in the afternoon chant and then returned to the non-stop cha-cha-cha of creation, preparing an Ottolenghi-inspired feast for the evening. I hoped people would be able to taste the universe, the mandala of flavours, the history of all they were about to taste.

I cooked quinoa, the sacred Inca grain, with its seven millennia of experience of nourishing people. The legend tells that when the Spanish first encountered the Inca people, they came across a strong, vigorous, well-nourished and resilient population. Every year, the Inca king was in charge of planting the first quinoa seed with a spade of gold. When the European invaders realised how important this crop was for the well-being of the people they were trying to conquer, they ordered every quinoa field to be burnt to the ground, and banned its cultivation. They also banned cocoa to the Aztecs, but that is another story. Without their wonder grain, the people weakened, starved and succumbed to illness, becoming the perfect slaves to be sent to the mines in search of precious metals.

Quinoa has been available in specialist shops for over a decade. It is so beautiful when it cooks; the little spirals begin to show themselves as the grain starts to swell. It tastes nutty, wholesome and succulent. I always rinse it first as quinoa is coated with saponin, which is bitter in taste. Saponin protects the grain from the ultraviolet rays of the sun in the Andean Hills where the best quinoa is grown. It also stops birds from eating it.

I cooked the quinoa according to the instructions on the packet and made a warm salad, adding strips of caramelised red onion, toasted pistachios, unsulphured apricots sliced in thin strips and orange zest. I added a squirt of cold pressed sunflower oil. I was cooking a feast and I was tired - Babette was beat - but the person that grew the quinoa probably works much harder than this every day of their lives, as do the spice collector and the orange grower. They plant and harvest as part of a circle, passing their harvest on to someone else to cook for another to eat. Honouring that circle is part of my practice. Here is the quinoa recipe. I served it with some of the pomegranate recipes that you will find in the next chapter.

Quinoa salad

Makes a large platter.

This is delicious as an accompaniment to tagines, and served with the aubergine dip. You can vary what you add to the salad: toasted pine nuts, chopped toasted pecans, pomegranate seeds, roasted vegetables, mint… all these work well. The idea is for you to have a base recipe, so that you can raid your cupboard and experiment! If you are lucky, you might be able to find red quinoa, which is so much nuttier and tastier.

2 cups quinoa
¼ cup shelled pistachios
1 medium red onion, sliced thinly
⅔ cup olive oil
Grated zest and juice of one orange
½ cup unsulphured dried apricots, chopped into strips
2 handfuls of rocket or baby spinach
A few basil leaves
Sea salt and freshly ground black pepper

Pre-heat the oven to 160°C. Spread the pistachios out on a baking tray and toast for 5 minutes, until the colour changes. Remove from the oven, allow to cool slightly, then chop roughly, but not too small. Set aside.

Rinse the quinoa well under cold running water until the water is clear, otherwise it can taste bitter when cooked. Put it in a pan with 2 cups of boiling water and simmer until all the water is absorbed. Spread it onto a flat tray and fluff the quinoa with a fork as if you were raking it, to allow air to get in. This accelerates the cooling process, and stops it overcooking.

Whilst the grains are cooking, fry the onion in three tablespoons of the olive oil in a small, heavy-based frying pan. Cook until it caramelises, over a low heat. This will take up to 15 minutes. Leave to cool in the oily mixture.

Soak the apricot slices in some of the orange juice, and make a dressing using the oil, the orange zest, salt and pepper and the rest of the orange juice.

In a large mixing bowl combine the quinoa with the dressing and the rest of the ingredients. Taste and adjust the seasoning. Serve at room temperature.

After supper, Simon asked me how many volunteers I needed for washing up. I usually ask for two, maximum three. I told him: "Nine please". There were only ten of us.

In the morning someone thanked me for last night's dinner and told me that the food was so delicious it made him weep, as he realised he would never taste that same meal again.

Chapter Thirteen
Pomegranates

Nightly she sings on yon pomegranate tree.

~ William Shakespeare, *Romeo & Juliet*

I use a lot of pomegranates in my cooking. I reintroduced them into my life a few years ago while choosing vegetables for a Western Zen retreat. I was at the greengrocer, collecting a bulky order for a week of cooking in the Welsh mountains, when I noticed a box of pomegranates. They were portly and round and stood out with their lustrous ochre glow, as if showing off all the sunshine they had accumulated in their lifetime. Even though I had no idea what I was going to do with them, I had to buy them. They joined me on my journey.

I suspect pomegranates of holding the secret of time travel. They transport me to specific moments of my childhood, not only with their flavour but in the whole experiencing of the fruit: the holding it, the looking at it, the knowing it. Pomegranate is known as the fruit of patience. It is sensual, curvy, the queen of fruit. She sits plump in the throne of her kingdom, boasting her frilly crown.

It is at its best in autumn, arriving in England from the Mediterranean and Middle East, China and North Africa, but you can buy it almost all year round. I love to sprinkle it in salads and to place it in meals where its seeds are least expected.

I often feel like I carry an invisible key ring with all the keys to places that were significant in my life. Certain things, smells, sounds, particularly in the meditative silence of a retreat, awaken the power of the keys and enable me to enter, like a visitor, those spaces in which I witness moments of a different time. It is here that I confront myself, where chunks of my life that were buried deep in my memory, locked up for decades, become vibrant and alive.

Pomegranates hold the key to my early years in calle Gregorio Gavier. My grandfather had bought two houses next to each other and had given one to my parents: he lived in one, we lived in the other. There was a door that connected the two houses. I liked his house. He had a piano and there was a pomegranate tree in the back garden. Its blossom used to attract tiny hummingbirds who came to feast on its nectar.

The neighbourhood children used to knock on the door and ask if the pomegranates were ready. When they were, our ritual started. We would pick them, bring them out onto the street, sit on the pavement and tuck in.

We loved to break the leathery rind, peel through the honeycomb membrane and rip into the juicy grains. Everyone ended up with hands, faces and clothes stained red; deep vermillion juice stained the pavement slabs around us like blood. Concentrating hard, we picked out the arils like edible rubies, piling them up in the palms of our hands. We avoided the white, unripe ones, and the yellow pith, we hated the bitter taste and the way it got stuck in your teeth. We stuffed the piles into our mouths, chewed, and sucked the juice out of them. We made slurping noises and some spat out the tiny seeds.

We sat on the pavement telling stories and eating. It was the only time the other kids allowed me to join in their games and I used to associate that glory of belonging with the flavour of teeth-made grenadine.

I tattooed a sweetheart with a bread knife on the trunk of that pomegranate tree. Inside it I carved the letter M. Matias was my third-grade boyfriend. We were both eight. I left the school at the end of that year, but I used to see him occasionally because he lived next door to my aunt's house on the other side of town. He was impish, an attention seeker, and he used to get up to all kinds of mischief. Perhaps it was because his father had died. One summer I went to my cousin's birthday party, where I joined crowds of girls in smock dresses and impeccable hair. Matias hadn't been invited, so he set fire to the tree at the front of the house. He used to wave shyly at me, peeping through a hole in the garden wall, his eyes a piercing blue. A few years later, as I was about to leave for school, I picked up the newspaper and read that a young boy had been shot dead in the city. Then I read the name: it was Matias. He and a friend had been playing in and around an abandoned house when a retired army captain, a neighbour, had fired a few shots to the air, allegedly in an attempt to frighten the boys away. A stray bullet hit Matias in the head and killed him. We were both twelve. The two next-door houses are still there, but I am sure they are no longer connected by a door. The pomegranate tree was knocked down after my grandfather died and his house was sold. But I still have the key. In my imagination, I still go and visit. I caress the bark of the tree; I see my grandpa smiling standing next to it and I still trace the letter M and the shape of the wonky sweetheart.

Roasted aubergines with pomegranates

I first came across this recipe in my brand new copy of Yotam Ottolenghi's cook book given to me by my friend Julia. It became a tradition to cook it towards the end of a retreat, as a treat. John Crook adored this dish. Now the book is my most battered, this recipe has evolved and I have my own take on it.

Serves 4

3 large aubergines cut into round, even slices (about 2 cm thick)
Plenty of extra virgin olive oil
2 tbsp toasted sunflower seeds
A handful of pomegranate seeds
A bunch of basil leaves

For the yoghurt dressing:

A small pinch of saffron strands
3 tbsp boiling water
180 g low fat natural yoghurt
1 garlic clove, crushed
Juice of 1 lemon
3 tbsp extra virgin olive oil
Sea salt

To make the dressing place the saffron in a bowl and add the boiling water. What you want here is colour, not for the strands to disintegrate. Leave to stand for a good five minutes. Toasting the saffron strands slightly beforehand will help diffuse the colour and flavour of this wonderful ingredient. I love watching as the water begins to change colour, the deep orange seeping out, like ink.

In a large mixing bowl, whisk the yogurt, garlic, extra virgin olive oil, lemon juice and sea salt. When the saffron water has cooled down, add it to the yogurt mixture and mix well. Leave in the fridge for the flavours and colours to intensify while you cook the aubergines.

Pre-heat oven to 220°C.

Place the aubergine slices on a roasting tray and toss them with plenty of olive oil, sea salt and pepper until each piece is coated, distributing them evenly. Roast for 20-35 minutes until the aubergines are cooked and have changed colour. They should be tender and have turned golden brown.

Once the aubergines have cooled slightly, place them in a pretty serving dish, cover with the dressing and, with your hands, scatter over the toasted sunflower seeds and the pomegranate seeds. Carefully tear each leaf from the basil stalk and arrange with the other toppings, making the whole dish look beautiful. Serve at room temperature.

Moorish aubergine dip

This dip is great for crudités, for accompanying couscous or quinoa salads and for serving with roasted vegetables. Fire is the key ingredient in this dip; the aubergine must be charred in flame to bring out its flavour.

1 aubergine
200 g natural yoghurt
2 tsp pomegranate molasses
Zest and juice of half a lemon
Drizzle of extra virgin olive oil
1 garlic clove
Sea salt

Hold the aubergine over an open flame (gas or wood) and allow it to burn evenly on all sides. You will need to stay with it, moving it around with a pair of metal tongs. Place in a bowl and cover with a plate. The aubergine will cool and the steam will make the peeling easier. To peel it, just slide your fingers from the tip to the end, making sure not to scrape the skin but at the same time removing all the charred bits.

Rub the garlic clove firmly around the surface of a mixing bowl, as if you were using a wax crayon to colour the inside of the bowl. This will give the dip a hint of aroma and flavour without overpowering it. Discard the leftover garlic. Put the aubergine, yoghurt and lemon juice into the bowl and use a potato masher to bind it all together. Add the pomegranate molasses and stir. Taste and season with sea salt. Add the oil and leave to rest. This dip is best served at room temperature.

Baba ganoush

1 aubergine
A pinch of sea salt
The juice of half a lemon
A handful of parsley
½ tsp pomegranate molasses

Char the aubergine and remove its skin, as in the previous recipe. Place the peeled, burnt aubergine in a bowl, add sea salt, lemon juice, freshly chopped parsley, olive oil and pomegranate molasses. Mash it all up into a paste and leave to rest before serving. It is great as a starter, eaten with white sourdough or toasted pitta bread. I also like to serve it alongside a big bowl of braised lentils (see recipe on page 82).

Autumn coleslaw

At home, we eat a raw, fresh salad every day. We have been growing our own vegetables since we arrived in York, so we eat freshly picked leaves for at least six months a year. The rest of the year, we try to resist succumbing to the bagged supermarket leaves, so our salads become crunchier, more entwined with the season. I love shredded cabbage and carrot, fennel, toasted seeds, but I dislike smothering it all with mayonnaise. It deflates the salad, taking its colour and lightness away.

This is a good basic recipe which you can change and adjust according to what you have in your fridge or vegetable box.

Serves 4

¼ medium red cabbage, finely sliced
¼ medium white cabbage, finely sliced
1 small fennel bulb, trimmed and finely sliced
4 small raw beetroots, very fresh, washed and finely sliced
3 carrots, peeled and coarsely grated
2 crisp apples, quartered, cored and finely sliced
1 small cup of pomegranate seeds
2 tbsp fresh lemon juice

For the dressing:

3 tbsp extra virgin olive oil
1 tbsp pomegranate molasses
1 tbsp cider vinegar
1 tsp Dijon mustard
½ tsp honey
Sea salt
Toasted sesame and pumpkin seeds

Carefully arrange all the vegetables and apples in a bowl. Drizzle over the lemon juice and toss, using your hands.

Whisk the dressing ingredients in a bowl until they blend. Add to the salad and toss well. Sprinkle over the toasted seeds and serve.

Chapter Fourteen

Retreat Seven: *Death of a Teacher*

It was January 2012, the beginning of a Silent Illumination retreat, led by Hilary. I sat in John's room, writing with John's pen. John felt present in each corner of this house. He had died in the summer, unexpectedly, and we were all still trying to come to terms with his death. I had cooked his last retreat at the Maenllwyd last February, where I had noticed how he beheld the landscape and the house, the surroundings. He contemplated them with a deep love, a oneness with the spirit of the place. He even managed to walk every day up the hill. His operation had given him the strength he had feared he would never regain.

Whilst planning a Tara puja, standing in the back yard, he had told me that he thought he would live for another ten years. John was the Maenllwyd and the Maenllwyd was John. How does a place that is so intrinsically connected with a person continue to be the same when that person is no longer there?

I remembered how his ashes danced in the wind, as his family scattered them at the top of the hill, near the lonesome tree. I heard his instruction as I gazed out of the window, full of sadness, yet with so much to do: "Get on with it!"

Meditation facing the wall in the evening, the wall as a mirror of me. An owl broke the silence ... hoot!

I had arrived feeling like a spectre: a sad, ghoulish me. January was doing its usual trick: trapping me in a spin of pain that drags me into a dark and petrifying space. It's as if a part of me dies in January, mirroring the landscape and the vegetation. All I wanted was to be in the Argentinian sunshine with my family. I longed for early morning breakfasts in La Granja, under the chinaberry trees, a round of maté tea at the long tiled table with baskets of bread and dishes of cold, salty butter.

I could hardly get out of bed to come. I took my time, drove slowly and arrived too late to make proper use of the few hours of precious daylight.

My mood snapped on arrival. I shifted from "barely functioning" to "so much to do, so many people to feed". The weather was unusually unwintry. The sun was shining.

John was everywhere I looked, I saw him sitting on the bench, mumbling that it wasn't cold enough. I missed him early in the morning, coming down the stairs for his first coffee fix of the day.

I had been kindly offered his room, which has a desk and lovely views. I felt grateful for the space. As I looked out of the window I could almost touch the mossy branches of the sycamore tree, which was confused by the unseasonal warmth, buds forming on each tip end.

The room was full of John's things: an oak desk with ring marks of mugs from an era gone; a silver and china tray holding two torches; an old box of matches; a pebble; some old batteries; a book of British birds and a small bread basket with his personal cards.

A couple of raggedy green coats hung from a hook on the ceiling, like a constant apparition. One was a green parka with a sheepskin collar, the other looked like a dressing gown: wool flannel with checked tweed details in the lapel and pockets, full of holes that only time and wear can make in garments.

I wondered if I shook them, would I shake out their tales? But as the day went on I realised that the stories were not in the dust; they were in the people who were carrying on what John started. John the adventurer, the seeker, the wizard, the teacher, reminding me through each object: "Get on with it!"

Tea beckoned. I made flapjack with jumbo oats and Welsh butter, melted with golden syrup, the zest of a navel orange, chopped, toasted walnuts and sea salt flakes. An offering.

Orange and pecan flapjacks

250 g golden caster sugar
250 g butter
425 g porridge oats
180 g golden syrup
50 g pecans
Zest of one organic orange (the skin of conventionally produced oranges is often laden with pesticides)

Pre-heat oven to 180°C.

Grease and line a shallow, 12 x 7 inch baking tin.

Toast pecans in a moderate oven, or in a heavy-based pan.

In a bowl over a pot of boiling water melt butter, sugar and syrup. Keep the temperature moderate, and stir constantly. Once the mixture has melted completely (if your bowl is big enough) stir in the oats, the toasted pecans, and the orange zest.

Mix well, pour the mixture into the tin and press it down, making sure it is level.

Bake for approximately 30 minutes, until the flapjack is golden but still soft. It is a good idea to mark the squares with a knife when the flapjacks are still warm as it makes them easier to slice once they have cooled down.

Rice is a wonderful and versatile grain, the main staple for so many millions in the world. I have experimented with many different types of rice on retreats: short brown, white basmati, brown basmati, Arborio and wild rice, to name but a few.

I decided to make a vegetable and rice bake, a dish that has evolved from a lumpy buckwheat bake I once ate at a Steiner School cafe. It is a recipe that changes all the time. Someone once asked me for the recipe but, after trying it out a few times, realised that it only worked when he focussed on the ingredients and followed his instincts, rather than follow specific instructions.

I used red Camargue rice, wild rice, oat groats, and spelt grain. They all have different cooking times, so you need to cook them separately; you can also use buckwheat, black Chinese rice, rye grain or brown rice. Each grain has its own nuttiness. I love making the dish as the process is almost ritualistic.

The secret is not to overcook the grains before they go into the oven. As I drained each type of grain I cooled it down before removing all excess liquid and mixing it in a bowl.

Separately, I slow-roasted cherry tomatoes, giving them time to caramelise and release lots of juice. All you need is olive oil and sea salt, and perhaps a bunch of rosemary or thyme.

I stir-fried, only slightly, so as not to lose bite, different vegetables: broccoli, carrots, red onions, red peppers, a little bit of chilli. You can use anything you like, as long as the vegetables have a variety of colours. I mixed the grains with the vegetables, and added fresh herbs: basil, parsley and tarragon. Then a good splash of tamari sauce, the juice from the tomatoes, and olive oil; the mixture has to be moist.

I toasted almonds soaked in tamari sauce, to make them salty and caramel-like, crunchy. I added those as well. Texture in this dish is important; there is a danger of ending up with a mush.

I mixed everything together, apart from the tomatoes, and poured it into a deep baking tray. The tomatoes went on top for decoration, along with some feta cheese and extra basil. It took about fifteen minutes to heat up, in a moderate oven. It is wonderful served at room temperature with a side salad.

Rain was falling heavily and grief was ever-present. The pace of the day was leaden. The ground was wet and seeping with springs which cut wounds through the grass. Everything was green and the weather mild. There was a sense of winter not having arrived yet. The holly tree which had suffered badly in the harshness of the previous winter did not seem to mind. Somehow it looked relieved, as did the birds playing hide and seek in the undergrowth.

I looked up as I was writing and saw the curtain of rain, bits of cloud, and a few dripping sheep staring at the valley below. Did the sheep know?

From my window I noticed a retreatant going around the place, fixing things. He had helped with the milk refrigeration system by tieing the crates and the bottles with blue rope, fixing the crates to the ground with stones and then placing them in the stream. He had changed the riddle wheel of the Rayburn before I arrived, replacing the old one with the forged cast iron wheel that I used to keep in the kitchen window to remind me that "the wheel of the teachings always turns". I had heard him howling this morning, outside the kitchen, and I could feel his grief mixing with mine; his pain like a mirror not only of my suffering, but of a collective, universal sorrow of loss.

I decided to try to enter fully into the sorrow, rather than push my emotions to one side. I knew that if I didn't confront it, it would take hold of me and drown me. I knew that I would find the necessary support from the teacher, Hilary, help from the trees, the mountain, the sky.

Hilary encouraged me to write. She told me to write about both the pleasant and the unpleasant, so I made a list describing how I felt before arriving here. I wrote three pages. Most was doom and gloom: "I feel flat, a desire to curl up and die, grief, voices in my head, self-pity, insomnia, drowsiness, exhaustion, blurry mind, awkwardness, disconnection, revulsion, nausea, despair, anger..."

How could I have allowed myself to get into this state? I noticed that as soon as I walked into the kitchen, I began to feel better.

As I stepped out of the kitchen and into the garden, a heavy drop of rain from the sycamore branch fell into the tiny bowl of soup sitting on the tray, a part of our lunch offering to Tara. I smiled. I noticed. I had strong fantasies of being transported to my grandma Fina's house. I longed to hear cicadas and green parakeets by the pool, and to eat a dulce de leche cake in the sunshine with my family. My mind went round in circles dreaming of magic carpets or winning the lottery. My husband Simon had in the past bought me a ticket at the last minute, when by mid January I was barely functioning. "Go and get your oxygen mask," he used to say.

Yet sometimes, on retreat, winter becomes comfort rather than penance or punishment. Could I drop the negative feelings and embrace "whatever comes"? I layered myself up with thermals, fingerless gloves, thick wool socks and sheepskin boots. Some of these clothes were older than my children. It was so dark in the kitchen that I also wore a head-torch most of the time.

Since I hadn't mastered magic or apparition I decided to offer people my home in a dish: a simple vanilla sponge with dulce de leche and coconut.

A lovely afternoon light fell on the valley at tea time. The colours dispelled the gloom and dug me out of the bog of ache. I breathed; and breath after breath, I opened up to now. I decided not to eat the evening meal, but I still took the tray with the offerings to Tara. The slugs were feasting on the freesia flowers I had left on the steps. Bugs hovered around my head torch and when I switched it off I noticed the full moon. I stood bathing in its light.

After dinner I walked across the yard towards the Chan Hall. A few people stood outside looking at the moon, which looked like a big circle of brilliant bread dough. As I took a few steps into the mud, clouds moved and two halos formed around the moon, a moon with a wreath of rainbows.

Hilary led us on a silent walk up the hill, in the quiet of night. There were no torches, only squelchy sounds of wellington boots sinking into the mud and a slow line of fifteen people walking at uniform pace in the pearly moonlight. The glow was glorious.

After the walk, I went back to my room, and became immersed in thoughts of tomorrow's menu. I lifted my head and looked out of the window and saw my reflection: my Fes scarf wrapped around my neck; a long braid falling on my left shoulder. I was wearing spectacles, green reading glasses I received for free when I bought the pair I keep in the kitchen. There was an ageing me in that reflection. One of the windows was slightly open and I saw my reflection merged with the sycamore branch, my face knotty and mossy, a Kahloesque picture of woman and tree.

As I shut the window the image of me was no longer split. My pen slid out of my hand. It was time to go and make the wheel of the Rayburn spin and riddle, to get the kitchen ready for the next day's potions.

I made a mushroomy miso soup. Miso is light but has substance. I always carry sachets of instant miso soup in my handbag. It comforts me better than a cup of tea.

There is always one day halfway through a retreat when people have had enough, or when things begin to shift. I call it the breakthrough day, or Miso Day. There is something about the clarity and goodness of miso that lightens the spirit.

Miso is a paste made from a fermented grain (usually soya), salt and *kōjikin*, a brewing fungus that has been used in Japan, Korea and China for over two millennia. Miso plays a key role in Buddhist monastic life in both Chan and Zen monasteries, nourishing teachers and monks. I use brown rice or barley miso to make soups; these are salty, so taste before you season. I sometimes put it in bread dough, and make black sesame miso rolls, or I add it to vinaigrettes, marinades and dressings. The possibilities are endless: become adventurous!

The secret of miso lies in not boiling it, as this affects its probiotic qualities and denatures the enzymes.

Miso soup

Serves 4

  ½ fresh chilli
  5 cm piece of fresh ginger
  1 stalk fresh lemongrass
  ½ leek
  4 small carrots
  ½ red pepper
  6 brown or shiitake mushrooms
  4 spring onions
  150 g green beans
  2 litres homemade vegetable stock
  4 -6 tbsp miso paste (to taste)
  1 tbsp tamari sauce
  Sesame oil
  A handful of fresh coriander

Finely slice the chilli, grate the ginger coarsely, cut the lemongrass in half and "bruise" it with the bottom of your chef's knife. Finely slice the leek. Grate the carrots. Cut the brown mushrooms into quarters, slice the pepper and the spring onions. Trim and finely slice the green beans.

In a heavy-based pan, fry the mushrooms in a little sesame oil, until they have softened. Lower the heat and add the tamari and the miso paste and mix well. Remove from heat and leave it to rest, then add the chilli, ginger and lemongrass and set aside for a couple of minutes.

Meanwhile, heat the stock in a new pot. Place it on the stove on a medium heat.

When the stock has boiled, turn off the heat and add the miso mixture. Mix well. Start to build your soup by placing all the vegetables in the miso soup and reheat it, making sure it doesn't boil. Place the lid on the pot and simmer for five minutes, making sure that the vegetables retain their colour.

Pour into four bowls and top with freshly chopped coriander and perhaps another dash of tamari sauce. A sprinkle of gomasio (see page 93) also works well with this soup.

After lunch, I started to heat the wok for the curry build-up. As I toasted black mustard and fenugreek seeds and fresh curry leaves, people kept peeping into the kitchen to check what was cooking.

Curry

This is my family's favourite curry. It springs from a Jamie Oliver recipe, and everyone knows how to make it now. Curry cooked from scratch is so different from one made with a ready-made sauce. Breathing in the aroma that comes from the first stage of toasting the spices is one of those deep experiences that make cooking sensual and transporting.

I have made this curry recipe, with variations, on almost every retreat. John often used to ask me if I could make it again on the last night. I serve it with my own take on a flat bread, somewhere between a chapatti and a naan bread, but I only do this if I have plenty of time as the breads need to be cooked one by one. I no longer follow a recipe when I make this curry and I suggest that you follow these instructions and then adapt it to your taste. Make it hotter or milder and try using other vegetables. Here I give instructions for either a butternut squash or a cauliflower curry.

Curry benefits from being left to stand so that the flavours intensify as the ingredients become acquainted with each other. On retreat I try to have the curry ready by the end of the rest period after lunch, only coming back to heat it up fifteen minutes before serving it for the evening meal.

Serves 4

1 butternut squash, peeled and cut into chunks, or 1 cauliflower
4 tbsp sunflower oil
2 tsp black mustard seeds

1 tsp fenugreek seeds
1 handful of curry leaves
1 fresh green chilli, seeded and thinly sliced
2 tbsp fresh ginger, coarsely grated
1 tsp turmeric
6 tomatoes, chopped (or a 400g tin of tomatoes)
14 oz tin coconut milk
Salt
A handful of cashew or pistachio nuts
A bunch of fresh coriander, chopped.

For the spiced rice:

Basmati rice
2 star anise
1 stick cinnamon
1 tbsp cardamom pods

Note on the chopping of vegetables for this curry:

In my opinion, onions should never be chopped in a food processor. It affects the consistency and almost destroys their *chi*, or energy. I cut the onions for this curry into long strips. First peel the onion, then cut it in half lengthwise. Slice as thinly as possible, following each line of the onion.

Chop the butternut squash into even, bite-sized cubes; after you seal them they should retain their bite and not disintegrate into a purée.

Cauliflowers are flowers and I treat them as such. I remove the leaves then gently tear the florets from the stalk. I never use a knife anywhere near the florets. You end up with a little mountain of tiny trees.

Find a heavy, stainless steel wok, or a heavy-based pan.

Pre-heat the oven to 160°C. Spread the pistachios or cashews out on a baking tray and toast for 8 minutes, until lightly coloured. Remove from the oven, allow to cool and set aside.

Heat some olive oil in the pan, add the butternut squash cubes and sprinkle with sea salt. The idea here is to seal the cubes, so that they are golden brown but they do not overcook. Use a medium to high heat and pay careful attention, keeping the cubes moving. When they are browned, reduce the heat and cover for five minutes so they sweat and cook a little more. Remove into a bowl and set aside.

Heat the pan again and start to dry toast the spices. First add the mustard seeds. Wait for them to pop, then add the fenugreek seeds and the curry leaves. Stir them, being careful not to burn them. Add the oil to the pan, followed by the chopped onions. Cook them until soft and translucent. Add the chillies and ginger. Stir and fry for a few minutes then add the turmeric. Chop the tomatoes in chunks, and add them to the curry. Cook for a couple of minutes, then add a cup of water and the coconut milk. Continue simmering and stirring. Season well with salt and taste the acidity as you might need a pinch of sugar as well. Remove from the heat.

Add either the sealed butternut squash cubes or the raw cauliflower florets to the base and allow the curry to stand, with a lid on, for as long as possible. Twenty minutes before serving, reheat gently and adjust the seasoning.

As you are about to serve, toss in the toasted cashews and the fresh coriander.

Serve with spiced steamed basmati rice. To cook the rice, heat a large pan and dry fry a couple of star anise, a stick of cinnamon and a tablespoon of cardamom pods. Once the pods start to make popping noises, add a tablespoon of oil, and the rice. I usually calculate one mug of rice for three or four people. Fry the rice lightly for 30 seconds and add 1¾ times the volume of rice to water. Add some salt, bring to the boil, cover the pan and reduce the heat as far as possible and cook for about twenty minutes. Brown rice has a much longer cooking time. When the rice is ready, scoop out the whole spices, which by then will have risen to the top. Fluff up the rice with a fork, and serve immediately.

Fresh fruit chutney

I make this fragrant chutney as an accompaniment to curry and I always tell people to serve on the plate with the curry and rice, rather than in a separate bowl. I make it with whatever tropical fruit I can find, remembering and honouring a simple lunch we were once treated to on Wasini Island, in Kenya. Use cantaloupe melon, pineapple, green papaya or mango. Try to make it at least a few hours ahead of serving. Sadly it does not keep very well, so eat it on the same day. Adapt the heat and sweetness to your own taste, but always use fresh chillies and coriander.

> 1 pineapple, peeled, cored and chopped into small cubes
> 1 ripe mango, chopped into small cubes
> 1 tbsp soft brown sugar
> A good pinch of sea salt
> Zest and juice of one lime
> Fresh coriander leaves, without the stalks
> 1 green chilli, pith and seeds removed, sliced finely
> Coconut flakes

Pre-heat the oven to 160°C. Spread the coconut flakes on a tray and bake until golden. Keep an eye on them as baking does not take much time at all. Allow to cool.

Toss the chopped fruit into a bowl, add the sugar, salt, lime zest and juice and the chillies. Mix well and allow to sit.

Check the seasoning, add the coriander leaves and the coconut flakes. Mix well and set aside until you are ready to serve.

I spent most of the miso and curry day crying, embracing my homesickness and my feelings of loss. It felt better to hold the ghosts rather than to fight them. I cradled them, soothed them with a sad song of sorrow. I sobbed throughout my afternoon nap, throughout the afternoon mantra chants, and again after the last mouthful of my supper. Yet the job still got done and the process kept on flowing.

The next day the sun came out after days of constant rain. I went for a walk up the hill, and when I got to the top, to the lonesome tree where we had scattered John's ashes, two red kites flew towards me and settled on one of its branches.

In the evening we did a fire puja by Green Tara. We walked slowly from the Chan Hall to Tara, carrying all the Tibetan instruments including a big drum John had left in his room with a tiny piece of paper: "Only to be used in very important Buddhist ceremonies." Pete blew the conch shell to the East, West, North and South, to the skies and finally to the earth. As the music faded, and the fire got going, we began chanting Guru Rinpoche's mantra, my favourite mantra, at lullaby pace: *Om ah hung benza guru peme siddhi hung.*

Hilary had asked us to write down something that we wanted to honour, or to let go of. We were then to burn it in the fire. I wrote something to remember: my first retreat, that first tasting of the universe. The way I opened up to the beauty of being. I wrote a note to myself: be your heart.

John's folding chair and hat had been placed by Tara. I only noticed it when the fire had almost gone out.

The weather had changed; the mood had also changed. During the morning work period I went out of the back kitchen to find one of the participants working on the lamps, wrapped in a scarf. He was soaked in sunlight, glowing, incandescent. A few minutes later Pete, the Guestmaster, came through the front door and said: "Go outside." Frost covered the valley like the fur of white foxes. It was lit by of the glow of the sun, which touched everything with warm red tones: flickers of auburn and ginger, ember-like. I stood in this moment of shining stillness, of hoarfrost and warmness. I went back inside and told people to stop chopping vegetables and go outside. As they stood gazing outwards a few had tears in their eyes, such was the beauty: devastating.

Instead of attending Hilary's talk, I sat and meditated in John's room. I lit an incense stick and waved it around, bowing, kindling the muses. The sun shone directly at me; it was just above the holly tree and the dormant lovage plant. It caught the little altar on the windowsill: a salt Buddha, pristine white. Sitting has been an important part of writing, of seeing, of dropping the distractions. I felt grateful and golden, my clothes tinted red by the sun. I felt just like an oat groat: organic, heartfelt, whole, nurtured.

Noticing is part of the process, not just cooking. Moments pass, minutes pass. Did you notice everything?

Did you notice the mint in the yogurt, the hint of clove on the braised lentils, the marigold petals? Did you notice the pain of the participants, did you feel it? Where? Did you notice how their faces changed as the retreat progressed?

Did you taste the fennel in the winter slaw, the hint of pomegranate in the dressing? The salt flake?

Did you wonder where it came from, who harvested it, packaged it?

Did you relish each bite like the only bite to be bitten, each chew, chewing, mindfully, that moment, gone, forever.

Did you notice the birdsong, just when you thought you could not go on, the birds, with their light feather coats, chirping in the cold? Why can't you sing like they do?

Did you see the sun rising over the frosted valley, the day opening, full of possibilities? Were you there or merely a spectator? Did you see the smouldering trees in all their nakedness? Did you see people's faces, distended and beautiful, and the barn ablaze, as if set alight?

Did you hear the owls? Were you kind? Did you do your job? Did you respect the man in his sorrow and pain? Did you notice the wisdom in his handwriting? Did you honour the kitchen, bow to the Buddha, light the incense with the tip of the flame, with reverence?

If you did, who was doing it? Where was your heart?

Chapter Fifteen

Ongamira

Ongamira, in the northwest of Cordoba, reminded my grandfather of Scotland. It was where we went for part of our summer holidays: we stayed in El Reposo, a hostel run by a Christian fellowship. Ongamira was a wild place. It had a surplus of sacredness, an enchanting landscape tainted with conquest and blood spill. The original inhabitants were Comechingon Indians, who were massacred by invading Spanish troops. The Spanish brought Jesuit monks with them, who built hundreds of miles of meticulous underground tunnels to connect their churches. The wild slopes that looked smooth from a distance were in fact mined with spiky pampas and paja brava, the ferocious grasses that made walking hazardous.

It is a place that still calls me and of which I have strong childhood memories. Good memories. I remember the steep, often misty, walk up the hill from El Reposo to La Puerta del Cielo (the name means heaven's door; it was named because of the altitude). I remember the haunted caves and grottos, the sound of cicadas and the damp smell of moist earth and pine needles in the woodland where we played. We used to pick wild mushrooms which we dried in the sun and kept in jars, destined for wintry slow-cooked tomato sauce. We used to sit around a green, icy pool, into which spring water gushed through a large iron tap. Only the fearless or the naïve ever jumped in.

We used to go out on horseback, on sheepskin saddles, which lay on top of woven rugs and blankets. When we were small we rode holding on to someone else; as we grew bigger and more audacious, we were given a horse to ourselves. We galloped and cantered on the meadows behind the lodge, feeling like explorers, following a trail upstream into the unknown.

165

My sister Magda was obsessed with horses and Pachi the caretaker sometimes used to lend her his horse in the afternoon. She would sit on a tree trunk outside his house for hours, waiting patiently. Often someone older would come and usurp her place, snatching the horse and with it, my sister's smile.

We came to Ongamira in the summer, at Easter and at Christmas, sharing the space with extended family and friends.

At Christmas time, Papa Noel used to appear in my grandpa's red pyjamas. We treasured our gifts of *suflair* chocolate from the kiosk. I remember sneaking into my older cousins' room and drinking *anana fizz*, a sparkling alcoholic pineapple drink that the adults allowed us to drink as a toast at midnight on Christmas Eve.

The house had big bedrooms that slept whole families, a communal dining area and a big kitchen with giant pots and a mysterious pantry. Our board and lodging included three meals a day; the cooking was basic, but full of heart.

There is only one memory that upsets me slightly. One New Year's Eve we took my grandmother Fina with us to Ongamira. As everyone toasted the New Year, in a big room full of people exhilarated with the prospect of new beginnings, I noticed that she was not there. She was sharing a room with me and my sisters and when I went looking for her I found her crying on my bed. My uncle Jorge had died the year before and she was overwhelmed by sadness. I sat with her and I remember trying to talk her out of it. It unsettled me to see her so upset.

When I was thirteen, a family we knew took over the management of El Reposo, and I decided to volunteer in the kitchen for a month during my school holidays. In exchange for help at meal times, setting and serving tables, and washing up, I got a shared room and all meals. Sometimes, if I was lucky, I got to help in the kitchen. The cook was feisty, a large woman whose name I can't recall. She ruled the roost like a fat hen and had the keys for the pantry. Often she was the only one allowed in it.

I can't really remember why I decided to go to work at El Reposo, rather than resting up from the exertions of school. I think I was curious and eager to spend time in the kitchen and I certainly wanted to make new friends. I suspect that I was drawn to serve others. I also fell tragically in love with a nineteen year old who treated me like a cute kid. A song called *Superheroes* by an Argentinian singer reminds me of that summer, of my teenage self:

> You are seeking instructions in how to cook books,
>
> you are mixing the sweet with salt,
>
> you acquire information from tin cans,
>
> you buy the whole world from a bazaar.

I felt very homesick. One weekend my parents came to visit, bringing a vanilla sponge with dulce de leche and coconut flakes, which my mum had baked with my grandma.

It was brought on a plate covered with a linen tea towel. I didn't share it with anyone and hid it under my bed. I ate it at night à la Nigella, making sure that the girl I shared the room with didn't see me. I wasn't being mean or greedy; I was just full of longing. The last crumbs became a feast for a group of red ants who ignored my possessiveness. I wonder if the ants got the same taste that I got: the familiar flavour of home, family and love.

Vanilla sponge with dulce de leche and coconut

110 g butter, at room temperature
110 g caster sugar
2 large eggs
110 g self-raising flour
½ tsp baking powder
1 tsp Madagascar or other good quality vanilla essence
200 g dulce de leche
20 g desiccated coconut

You will need two 7 inch sponge tins at least 2 inches deep, greased and lined with greaseproof paper.

Pre-heat the oven to 170°C.

In a medium-sized mixing bowl, cream the butter and sugar together until you get a pale, fluffy mixture that drops off the spoon easily. In a separate bowl, beat the eggs thoroughly, then add them a little at a time, beating well after each addition. Beat in the vanilla essence.

When the eggs and vanilla essence have been incorporated, take a metal tablespoon, which will cut and fold the flour in much better than a thick wooden spoon. Sift about a quarter of the flour and baking powder onto the mixture and gently fold in. Repeat until all the flour is incorporated. Lifting the sieve high above the bowl will ensure that the flour gets a good airing before it reaches the mixture.

You should have a mixture that will drop off the spoon easily when you tap it on the side of the bowl. If not, add a little hot water. Now divide the mixture equally between the prepared tins. Place them on the centre shelf of the oven, and check after 15-20 minutes.

When they are cooked, the centres will feel springy when you touch them with your finger, and no imprint will remain. Remove them from the oven. After about a minute or so, turn them out on to a wire cooling tray, loosening them around the edges with a palette knife first. Then carefully peel off the base papers and leave the cakes to cool completely.

Spread some dulce de leche onto the base of a plate, and place one of the cakes directly on top. Sandwich the cakes together with a generous amount of dulce de leche.

Ice the top and the sides with more dulce de leche and sprinkle with the coconut.

Chapter Sixteen

Retreat Eight: *Countless Jewels*

At four in the morning, I heard a racket of bird noise coming from the branches of the hollow sycamore underneath my window at the Maenllwyd. It was a raucous quarrel between magpies and jackdaws, a skirmish of scavengers. I knew it would be pointless to try to go back to sleep; the clappers would sound in an hour. At five, I duly heard the Guestmaster going around the house, waking everyone up, and I layered on woollens and scarves and ran downstairs to boil the kettles. I felt happy to be here: it was a special retreat. Last year's *Mahamudra* was John's last retreat in the Maenllwyd and I was pleased he had left Sophie to continue leading this retreat in the Tibetan tradition. *Vajrayana* or *Tantra* is the form of Buddhism which comes to us from Tibet. Tantra means "continuity", meaning both the unobstructed presence of the sacred within all things and the practices which maintain the bright flow of awakening to this.

We were a small group. At the last minute Jin Ho, a Taiwanese nun studying in England, decided to stay for the week after popping round to say hello. I had met her before and we had shared some special times together. She follows a monastic diet, which excludes onions, garlic, leeks, spring onions and chillies. I had cooked for Jin Ho before and I was always honoured to cook her special meals. There were only three kitchen assistants but we would manage.

For lunch I served a fragrant celeriac soup with spelt rolls. I had expected spelt to be a difficult flour to work with but the rolls turned out crusty, light and airy.

In the afternoon we held a ceremony in the Chan Hall for our dear friend Alec, whose funeral was taking place at around the same time. Sophie led the chanting and we lit a piece of frankincense, a gift from Alec to Hughie. I was still in shock at this untimely loss of a dear friend, finding it difficult to grieve. As the incense stick began to burn and smoke, I thought of Alec and his perfume stories. He was an outstanding perfumier, with a passion for smells and taste. He used to tell me stories of the ancient frankincense trade, of the times when its sweet aromatic smoke used to be considered precious, and of how it is extracted from the boswellia tree. The tree is stripped, the bark is lacerated and the resin bleeds out of the tree and becomes firm. When the resin becomes hard it is called tears. The incense became a symbol of the tears I was not able to shed despite my sense of loss.

The daffodils were still blooming and the sycamore buds were tentatively opening. Baby lambs hopped about in the surrounding fields and the lovage plant was lush.

I made the mushroom stew using some young, flavoursome shoots of lovage. I used scissors to cut them off the plant, very carefully, to allow the plant to continue growing.

I noticed a big tub of organic pearl barley in the pantry and decided to serve it with the mushrooms. Apart from tossing some grains into minestrone soup I had never cooked with it. I stood next to the pot as it boiled, as I was not sure about the cooking time. After about twenty minutes, I tasted it. It was cooked but still firm so I drained it and allowed it to cool slightly. It looked lovely: sheeny white with a dark line across the grain.

I made far more than we needed for supper; this gave me something to be creative with the following day.

Barley's origins are traced to ancient Mesopotamia and it is considered to be the oldest cultivated grain. A relative of the rice plant, traces have been found in Neolithic Middle Eastern sites dating from around 8000 BC.

Although it has largely been replaced by wheat and rye in Europe since the Middle Ages, it is still a vital grain in many parts of the world due to its weather resistance and adaptability. It is an important food for Tibetans; in Japan it is used to make tea and miso. The Scots still use it in scotch broth and in the production of whisky. It is nutritious and low in fat. If you roast barley before cooking it, it has a nuttier taste and cooks much faster.

The barley complemented the mushrooms well: little piles of pearls on people's plates, seeping up the inky juice from the stew.

Because of the season, the mountain was hosting not only the retreat participants but dozens of sheep and their brood: the spring lambs who hopped away and hid when I approached them. They were daringly shy, their woolly coats marked with neon graffiti, sapphire symbols sealing their fate even before they were fat enough to satisfy the greed of Sunday roast lovers. Life auctions them at birth with a spray can.

I loved their bleating sounds, their call of Maaaaa. I sat and watched them play in small gangs, like scamps rampaging down the bank. Some hiding, others seeking, they ran and chased each other. On the other side of the track I watched the mothers graze in peace, their swollen teats resting from the tear and suck of their young.

The next day, the pearl barley became a salad to accompany a sweet potato tagine. I cooked half a cup of wild rice and mixed it with the barley, slowly caramelised some red onions, toasted some pistachios, sliced apricots and added a curl of orange zest and some fresh basil. I made a dressing with extra virgin olive oil, balsamic vinegar, orange juice and sea salt. I added just enough to give it some moisture.

The weather was unseasonably cold, too cold. I wore three pairs of socks, but my feet still sought warmth from any source of heat I could find: from the lumps of coal in the pit of the stove; from the open fire; from the gas heaters. It was warmer outside than it was in the house.

The squirrel who lives in the tree by the compost heap looked as if she had had a good winter. She was so fat that she struggled on her runs to pilfer bits of food from the offering tray; she would soon make a tasty treat for hawks and owls. Perhaps she was pregnant.

I felt quite detached from the group. Jin Ho gave me a head and neck massage using almond oil mixed with natural scent oils Alec gave me: benzoin, labdanum, rose Otto. She was kind and caring and told me to relax. My arms ached; I had a ball of trapped nerves in the back of my neck, at the level of my throat. It felt like an accumulation of things left unsaid, of my untruths.

Jin Ho always appeared when I needed her most. I remember arriving to cook for a Western Zen Retreat one spring, on the day she finished a three-month solitary retreat in the little hut in the grounds of the Maenllwyd. She had spent the winter there, and decided she would like to stay another week. She asked me if I would cook her one meal a day; in return she would come and help me in the kitchen. We took a walk together every afternoon, leaving the teapots and cake ready for the retreatants. We would stroll in a full circle, up and down the valley, sharing stories and questions. Sometimes we just walked in silence.

As we walked and talked I was struck by her child-like face, her unwrinkledness. I sensed her ease with the world, her eyes full of wonder and mischief. She embodied clarity, serenity and a different kind of happy: an established contentment. It was during that retreat that I felt in my heart that I wanted to be a Buddhist, not as a religion, but as a path to achieve some of the serenity I saw in her.

One day, back on that retreat, as I was making a vegan chocolate cake in the morning, I asked her if there was anything she really wished she could eat after three months away from the world. She said "chips", so I made her a nice plate of chunky chips for her lunch.

Vegan chocolate cake

200 g self-raising flour (preferably wholemeal)
200 g soft brown sugar
4 tbsp cocoa powder
1 tsp bicarbonate of soda
½ tsp salt
5 tbsp sunflower oil
1 tsp good quality vanilla extract
1 tsp distilled white vinegar
250 ml water

Pre-heat oven to 180°C. Lightly grease and line an 8 inch round cake tin.

Sieve together the flour, cocoa, bicarbonate of soda and salt, and stir in the sugar. Add the oil, vanilla, vinegar and water. Mix together until smooth.

Pour into the prepared tin and bake for 45 minutes. Remove from oven and allow to cool. If you like, you can make some frosting or dust it with cocoa.

On the last full day of that retreat, Jin Ho invited me to her hut for some green tea. What hit me was the frugality. She had spent three months in this woodshed with a bed, a book, a stove, her *mala* (Buddhist prayer beads), her coat and a pair of snow boots. There was so much freedom in this austerity, no stuff to tidy or put away, no clutter. We sat and drank tea and thanked each other for the few days we had shared.

Despite my headaches, the food that came out of the kitchen was full of flavour and flair. The three assistants were focussed and diligent. One rainy day, I joined the group for a meditation in the Chan Hall. I visualised countless jewels healing my tensions. The weather was typical of April in Wales: rain, clouds, sunshine, and a chill in the air. It was a common occurrence to see rainbows lying above the valleys.

In the afternoon after tea, we offered a sacred chant, invoking the many different qualities of Guru Rinpoche, conjuring his presence and literally inviting the Guru to "dance" among us: calling him with mantra and sacred Tibetan instruments, both to the room itself and into our hearts. Guru Rinpoche (or *Padmasambhava*, which means Lotus-born), was John's *yidam*, or meditational deity, a guardian and protector. Sophie read from a talk by John telling the story of how Guru Rinpoche had brought Buddhism to Tibet in the eighth century. I giggled as I heard John's words, remembering how fascinating his talks and stories used to be. We all laughed, and I am sure that those in the room who knew him were missing him terribly at that moment. We decided to do a little music practice, with all the instruments, and make "celestial music". I played a long *dung chen*, a very long wind instrument that makes a low and powerful sound, like the sound of an elephant. Others played bells and drums, a conch shell and a horn made from a human thighbone. We made a racket. That was the point: the chaotic discordance was beautiful and organic.

Once again, we chanted Padmasambhava's mantra, *Om ah hung benza guru peme siddhi hung*, at lullaby pace. I found myself weeping. It awakened something visceral in me, a kind of primitive mourning. It also felt healing. The word atonement came into my mind, *at-onement*. The wind blew into the room; the weather became agitated. Later came the first hailstorm. Hailstones like tiny gems covered the ground, countless jewels making the birds shiver.

I returned to get supper ready with a strong sense of John's presence, my heart full of gratitude for having had the privilege of having known this great teacher. I gave thanks for the hail and for the rainbows, for the rain and the sunshine.

If I were to describe a "Zen" moment with a vegetable on retreat, it would probably be with beetroot. Beetroots have a bad press, as they often get overcooked or overpickled. This sweet, earthy root is eager to offer itself to the cook for some creative treatment. Buy it fresh in bunches, making sure it is firm to the touch. If you are lucky you might be able to find a variation on the burgundy-red variety, such as the stripy Chioggio, or golden-yellow and orange or light pink ones.

I love baby beets from the allotment, boiled for ten minutes straight after picking with just a bit of salt. You can add them to a salad of mixed leaves whilst they are still slightly warm; the beets melt in your mouth, tasting of earth and sweetness.

On retreats where I have electricity I make a lovely beetroot dip. I also make beetroot hummus and take beetroot on journeys with other vegetables. It is wonderful with orange, fresh baby spinach leaves and crumbly feta, and it loves tamari sauce.

Beetroots work best when roasted. Peel them and cut them first in half across making sure you have even sizes. Using your hands, coat them with olive oil and a little tamari sauce, and roast them for at least half an hour at 180 degrees. Don't overcook - they must still have bite.

Beetroot dip

This dip needs firm, uncooked beetroots. It has always been a winner whenever I have made it. It was inspired by a mezze in Skye Gyngell's first cookery book, *A Year in My Kitchen*, which I treasure.

1½ - 2 kg beetroot, cooked and peeled (you can either roast or boil them, but don't overcook them)
1 garlic clove, peeled
½ large red chilli, deseeded.
A small bunch of fresh coriander
½ bunch of mint, leaves only
1 tbsp roasted spice mix
3 tbsp good quality balsamic vinegar
2 tbsp extra virgin olive oil
125 ml thick Greek-style yoghurt
Sea salt

Place the beetroot in a blender with the garlic and chilli. Pulse, then add the rest of the ingredients. The dip should not be too homogenised, try to let it keep a grainy texture. Put into a bowl, cover with olive oil and serve at room temperature.

For the roasted spice mix:

2 tsp fennel seeds
2 tsp mustard seeds
1 star anise
1 small cinnamon stick
2 tsp coriander seeds
2 tsp cumin seeds

Put all the spices into a heavy-based pan over a low heat. Shake the pan to mix and toast them, and do not leave them unattended. When you begin to hear popping noises, turn the heat off and allow them to cool. Grind them into a powder in a pestle and mortar and store in a jar.

The slugs appeared on Tara's steps: for the first time, I felt totally present on the retreat. They left sparkly traces on the stone, diamond slime that glinted for the few moments that the sun shone in the early morning.

The ferns that grow everywhere around the house were beginning to show; embryo-like sprouts of new life emerging in furry curls. Some of the fronds looked like centipedes, others like alien ram horns.

During one of the work periods, the sky darkened suddenly and bellowed with thunder. A heavy hailstorm descended upon the valley, the temperature dropped, and a white sheet of satin-like nuggets of ice fleetingly covered the ground once more.

I lit flames and fed fires and the Rayburn felt greedy as I poured coal into her pit. I asked her to give me more, and she did: she roared and the kettles danced and jumped, spitting water that sizzled as it hit the hotplate. The kitchen felt boisterous: the lamps hissed; the aubergines splattered in hot olive oil.

I decided to make a veggie roast, which was unusual for me. I had never been too keen on nut roasts but there was a big bag of mixed chopped nuts in the pantry and I thought I would give them another try. In January I had made little nut cakes with roasted vegetables and some wonderfully fat capers from Puglia that one of my friends had salted and stored in tiny jars and had brought as a gift to the kitchen. On that occasion I failed miserably to make them moist, and the Guestmaster told me I should have made gravy.

I toasted the nut mix in a tray in the oven, being careful not to burn it. It went from pale-white to honey-gold.

I caramelised a red onion, chopped a parsnip into small bits and threw in some tiny cubes of green pepper. I added fresh basil, parsley, salt and pepper and quinoa puffs instead of breadcrumbs, as a few of the retreatants didn't eat wheat. I mixed all this with the nuts in a bowl and added olive oil and four eggs. It probably needed more, but that was all I had.

I let the mixture sit, so that the ingredients had time to soak each other up. With help from one of the kitchen assistants, I shaped the mix into balls which I placed in muffin cases. They went into the oven at 180 degrees until they turned golden brown.

I served them with slow-roasted garlic potatoes, onion gravy with tamari and a lovage sauce. Perhaps the sheep across the field would bow to us in gratitude if they knew. Who needs lamb when you can have such a moreish roast. The offering I left on the steps was devoured overnight.

Tantra awakens my senses, it makes my heart beat fast. At five thirty the following morning, dawn was breaking. The green of the sheep's pasture had a pistachio tone: bright, like a raw nut. The patches of peat and bracken where the sheep would breakfast were glowing with the first sunrays. The lambs were still asleep, curled up in pairs. The rain had finally ceased and everything was soggy. The prayer flags around the trees dripped heavy drops.

That night we did another puja, this time for *Chenrezig*, the Bodhisattva of compassion. The room was transformed into a ceremonial circle, and we offered gifts in beautiful crystal glasses and bowls. The Chan Hall glowed.

We chanted the offering mantra (for gifts), which included a *mudra* (a movement of the hands). We offered gifts that correspond to the welcome attention a host in ancient India would give to a guest. There were eight offerings: water for drinking; water for washing dust off the feet (which was collected from the stream); flowers; incense; light; perfume; music and food. We made the perfume with fragrant almond oil mixed with saffron. As food, we offered rice, pulses and spices, and music was offered in the form of a Tibetan conch shell. We finished late and I slept with a clear heart. I had reconnected, through ritual, with the vastness and simplicity of being.

Before I started cooking at the Maenllwyd, I had forgotten who I was. In the turmoil of life, of growing up, of leaving, in the pain of heartbreak and separation, of parenthood, of busy life and money worries, the essence of me had disappeared somewhere deep. I had gone into hiding, too vulnerable perhaps, too frightened. It felt like a part of me had wilted. I was living in exile within myself. I found cooking a revelation. The more I got lost in the process of cooking, the more at home I felt. Memories were re-awakened by smells and flavours. I realised that my soul had been nurtured through food, in kitchens, with the women of the family, on church retreats, at long tables under shady vines, with friends, in different parts of the world, with my children.

The power of that simple, rustic kitchen threw me back into the flow of Flo. It offered me no time to dwell or indulge, just this sensuous state of knowing, of trusting a connection with something deep within myself. It was a call of the wild, where the inner goddess of creation arose to join the other participants: the cooker, the Rayburn, the kettles. I learned to dance, with reverence, with the fruits of the earth, with fire, water, wood and stone.

On the mountain I meet with spirits. Their ancestral presence unravels as I pour myself into the duties of the day. They come by night in the hoot of an owl, in the breeze entering my sleeping space through the half-open window in the Buddha room.

They come because I invoke them with silence and ritual. They descend and erupt from within me and around me, from the bog of my memories, the infinite accumulation of unspoken treasure. They float from the valleys, descend from the hills, and I am open to them. It is like opening a door to endless possibilities.

As I pour some oil into a pan, still unsure of what the soup is going to be, something rises from within, a knowledge that transcends rational knowing, that what to do next is in me all the time, yet it flows only when I am silent and connected with what I am doing. It flows as my hand takes a pinch of salt from the bowl and sprinkles it into the pot, before I add the chopped onions.

Cooking on retreats in the Maenllwyd is where I come to connect with myself, and with the larger "self" of the universe. I come to the home of the non-linguistic me, to connect with something that is unspoken, guttural, a residue of learning and yearning, the whispered secrets of family language, ancestral storybooks never written, an archaic wisdom that goes beyond purely cognitive knowing. A form of knowing takes over, one which is instinctual, powerful, which works best if I just let it flow, without dwelling on it or attempting to understand it. We are a store room of stories untold, of encyclopaedias of facts that are not empirically shaped. And it all unravels while I am stacking pots, arranging bowls, observing that the measuring jug has got a crack yet it does its job. Despite no longer having the riddling wheel standing against the window, as part of my kitchen shrine, I get the strong sense that the wheel of the teaching always turns, it fuses what we learn and what we have known all along. What is it that makes us forget? Meditation is a practice of remembering what we are and what we have lost or forgotten along the way.

In the Zen kitchen, scales and measurements are secondary. Instinct and connectedness are the key ingredients, together with heart. This knowing does not come from a book, but if we are still, silent, meditative and eager to create, something clicks, unstitches into a more powerful sense that leaves the books standing on the shelf. Zen cooking is about experiencing each moment, being aware of our presence but also the presence of everything else we are working with, who we are cooking for.

Art and beauty are everywhere and there is nothing more perfect than nature. To understand beauty you must understand what it means to be alive: fleeting, complex and wonderful. Alive and aware, in love and communion with everything.

Chapter Seventeen

Butterfly

A September morning, and I was cooking for another retreat at Bala Brook. A blue tit chirped from the rhododendrons, the kettle whistled, the Aga was hot. I opened the tins of tea. The next break in the meditation schedule would be a short one so I decided to make only three types. I was in the mood for Oolong, because I had learned recently that it meant "black dragon tea". I picked Darjeeling for its musky taste and caramel tint. I also made Rosehip with two tea bags and at the last minute I dropped a few Rain Flower green tea strands into the last pot. I watched as they swelled in the hot steamy water.

With a busy day ahead, I started on a few preparations. The morning's chanting resonated in me as I stirred the soup stock, chopped some mint, and sliced warm bread. The chanting (of an ancient Buddhist text, the *Heart Sutra*) soothed ancient sorrows from my heart, from my parents' hearts, from the heart of all humanity.

Here I was again: the Cook at Bala Brook. The garden was overgrown and the bounty of late summer lay at my feet: fruit-laden trees; herb borders attracting bees and bugs; marigold and borage flowers drying on the windowsill waiting to sit atop the icing of the afternoon cup cakes.

I found solace in the solitude of the meditative kitchen. I felt like a prisoner whose blindfold was being carefully removed after years of captivity. My eyes were slowly readjusting to the light, beginning the process of re-focussing in order to see again. After all that time of darkness and blurriness, things began to appear. As I opened up to the world, so the whole world opened up to me.

I was beginning to see again with the same eyes I had when I was a little girl: that way of seeing with wonder. The colours around me intensified, everything moved me. The wasps losing their nest on the landing window, a pair of dragonflies mating: I observed them for a long time, how beautiful and furry, how in "it" they were. The Japanese berry tree behind the house changed colour by the hour; the knotted oak swished in the gentle breeze. The stream kept up its constant chanting: water flowed, the kitchen flowed, time became me and I became time.

Once again, I had been given a question to work with: "What is this?"

What is this thing that came to Bala Brook?

What is this boulder trying to flex into diamond?

Why is this body so disconnected from this person?

Why can't I ever feel that obvious perfection of the simple fact that I am alive, that I am made of the same material as everything else in the universe, that I am pure stardust, that I am more alive than Venus?

As I went to light a candle in the early morning I found a dead butterfly on the windowsill. Its legs were crossed over its chest, solemnly compliant to the death that had befallen it.

As I picked it up, the powdery vestige from its wings tinted my fingers with orange fairy dust. How fleeting is the life of the butterfly. It has no time to dwell, no concern. A butterfly is not aware, a butterfly just is. Life and death do not differ from egg, larvae, pupa. It is all one thing and yet, when I look at how perfect it is, I become lost in the moment, becoming part of the grace of its short, ephemeral lifespan, stirred by the beauty in its unknowing of it.

Once the moment had passed, I had a sense of my own splendour and fragility, as the butterfly lay in the palm of my hand. I decided to go out into the garden to collect leaves and conkers: I would make the butterfly the centre of an offering to the Sri Lankan shrine in the entrance hall. In the meantime, I placed the butterfly in the joined hands of the White Tara statue in the kitchen.

I went out into the sun, chanting Tara's mantra to myself, those special words that have been chanted by generations of devotees: *Om tāre tuttāre ture svāhā*. My heart expanded with gratitude to the butterfly. I walked around the garden, in awe of everything that is alive. I could hear the stream but I could also hear my heart beating. I caressed the rocks, picked some red leaves and shook the borage plant so that some of its bluest flowers would drop into my hands. I collected weed seeds. My feet were bare, my limbs loose. I found myself walking in time to the Sanskrit mantra. With my small basket of gifts for the butterfly, I lingered on the bench by the brook's edge. I knew that lunch needed to be served soon, but also that this was the right moment to do exactly what I was doing.

Chapter Eighteen

Retreat Nine: *Transformation*

L ike a whirlwind I packed the car and left York with my foot pressed down on the accelerator, looking forward to the retreat. As I drew closer to the Maenllwyd, I noticed that I was anticipating what I often dread: I carried a strong desire to dive into the process. The journey was like any other past journey: the car packed with ingredients, each nook and cranny filled with bunches of herbs, boxes of tea and jars of crunchy peanut butter. What had changed? Perhaps it was me who was different? I was still processing the note to myself that I had written only a month before when everything seemed doomed: "Be your heart."

As I opened the first gate, in the distance I saw smoke coming out of the Chan Hall's chimney and a few cars parked in the yard. I stood and soaked it up, not just as a mere bystander.

Four or five people were already there. All men; I was in the company of wolves. There had been some further changes in the house since John's death: a new pine dresser cut in half, as the ceilings are low. The shelves were perfect for displaying teapots and jugs.

I was here to unravel a new story, to re-tell my tale. I asked the teacher if I could once again work with the first question I had ever worked with on retreat: "Tell me who you are."

The kitchen flowed from the moment I stepped into it, to the rhythm of my heart. People flocked to the kitchen to offer help and even before the retreat started, everything was in place: flowers in vases, tables laid and ready for breakfast. A big stainless steel pot full of fruit compote boiled away on the stove. A retreatant who knew about my connection to the slugs came and told me that he felt sad that it was winter and that they might not appear. In my heart I knew that they would, but I kept this to myself. I had brought a bunch of hyacinths; one of its tiny fragrant flowers would draw them out.

As we sat by the fire with a cup of tea, each person shared their story of why they had come. People felt a little apprehensive: the gate was closed, and we were in. Each told a little story of why they were here; it was our last chance to chat for a while. There were some familiar faces, others new. The next day, each person would begin their own solitary process, engaging with their koan, the meals and each other. The plate of biscuits suddenly contained only crumbs.

Meals at the Maenllwyd are traditionally served by the teacher, but Eddy, who was leading the retreat, had asked me to do it instead. He wanted me to be in charge of the food. At first I was taken aback, honoured to be asked but uncomfortable with the break in tradition. I realised that I did not want to miss out on my daily visits to Tara, so I asked Peter if he would serve.

Eddy had also asked me to explain the washing up ritual. I had been waiting for this opportunity for a long time: the ceremony of washing up at the tables, passing hot water from person to person, had captivated me from the first meal I had eaten at the Maenllwyd. Each person pours hot water into their bowl and mug, and rinses any remaining bits of food or drink into a large central bowl. There is so much to be learned in the simplicity of the task: a ceremony of mindfulness and gratitude. It is a silent and humble process. After each meal the dirty water from the central bowls, containing the remnants of the food, is offered to the hungry ghosts. In Tibetan Buddhism, hungry ghosts are spirits who roam their realm in terrible suffering. They experience hunger and thirst and live in constant fear. They have very narrow throats and huge stomachs and they can only be fed water with small crumbs of food. In some Japanese monasteries, only the rice water is offered to the hungry ghosts, as anything larger could become wedged in their throats. Some people fear hungry ghosts; I can only feel compassion and sadness for them.

I shared this story with the group, and suggested that those who found the idea of hungry ghosts too far-fetched should think about the constant hunger, thirst and fear experienced by millions of people in our earthly realm.

The next morning, I started making the bread straight after breakfast, leaving the dough to prove whilst I went to Eddy's first talk. He shared a story I really liked: There was a Zen master named Mazu who used to sit in meditation all day long. One day his teacher Nanyue approached him and asked, "Great monk, what do you intend by doing meditation?" He meant to check up on his real motivations, since Mazu seemed the perfect Zen student - too perfect, in fact. Mazu replied, "I am intending to be a Buddha."

At this, Nanyue picked up a brick lying on the ground and began to polish it. Mazu stared at him and said, "What are you doing?"

Nanyue said calmly, "I am trying to make a mirror."

Mazu said, "How can you make a mirror by polishing a brick?"

Nanyue looked at him and replied, "How can you become a Buddha by doing meditation?"

When the talk finished I ran back to the kitchen to begin working on the bread dough again. Eddy's words resonated as I sank my hands in the airy bread mix, listening as the bubbles of air deflated. Who was I? Making a mirror, becoming a Buddha, can it be done while making bread? These were questions with no answer, just small glimpses of realisation. From packets of dry ingredients scattered around the kitchen, to water, to dough, to giving something shape and form, to the moment I removed the tray from the oven, smelled the bread, tapped the base to check if it was ready. The question remained with me as I brought the warm bread to the table, and saw people's faces and the butter melting on the warm crust.

I cooked the usual first meal of inky mushroom stew and polenta and served it with a green salad of crisp lettuce leaves, rocket and little gem. I made a dressing with white balsamic vinegar, wholegrain mustard, runny honey and a handful of pink peppercorns crushed in the pestle and mortar.

I lit Padmasambhava's altar in the refectory and sang his mantra at lullaby pace, thinking of John and of my feelings of loss. The pain had receded a little. My voice sounded clear and melodic as I lit the heaters to warm the drafty room.

Everyone came to eat with their coats on: the house would take a few days to warm up. The wood burning stove was difficult to light, but I tried to keep it going. The room looked lovely with the chandelier lit and candles at the altar: dim and welcoming, magic almost.

After supper I took a cracked crystal bowl and filled it with tea lights and a hellebore flower I had picked from my garden. I made an offering to Tara for my women friends: it was an offering of gratitude for the restoration of my relationships with women and with my own femininity. It was a cold, wet night. The steps were slippery as I stepped onto them, singing Tara's mantra, wearing three scarves. The last step was packed with slugs, eating the roll I had baked that morning, and feasting on the tiny pale blue hyacinth flowers.

I felt so happy. Slugs are the antithesis of radiance: they eat the buds and shoots of the plants I love the most. Yet here, at Tara's steps, I connected to the spirit of the slug, letting go of my previous story of dislike. By dropping the story, I was able to connect with its spirit, its slugness, and therefore with the spirit of everything. The slug had become a symbol of love and the heart of that which I nourish and feed and invoke. Slugs appeared out of nowhere, on a chilly winter's night, when they were least expected. I saw how feeding the slugs had been a ritual, one which I started with no aim. It had been a tantric process of feeding them because they were there, because I saw them, the creatures with no face. As I connected with them, I was able to connect with myself too. The slug had become a metaphor of me; the process of coming here to cook my life was like the orchids I fed to myself.

I joined everyone in the Chan Hall in the evening for a communication exercise. Staring into each other's eyes, we asked each other's question. My heart filled up with love for the stranger sitting in front of me.

He asked me: "Tell me who you are." I am my heart. I am a woman tired of being a little girl, a good little girl. The girl has grown up because I have helped her heal.

I am a goddess connected with my spirit and with the spirit of everything. I embrace rituals; they help me maintain the state of bliss. Thoughts arise: I observe them, nod at them, let them through, let them go. I connect with the ample realm of the universe; ask for help, for permission. I ask my ancestors, what can I do to help?

I am sensing, opening, flowering. Seeing with my heart, I am my heart. I am covered in rose petals: rose petals the colour of blood.

I am a revolution, a rebel brewing.

I jumped out of bed at 5 am with an energy that felt new to me. In the distance I heard my mind telling me to lie in for five more minutes, but it weakened as I ignored it. I couldn't wait to check the Rayburn and warm the teapots. I threw some clothes on and ran downstairs.

Dawn broke the clouded sky: birdsong, stream, a change of light. Both the day and I felt full of potential.

During a rest period Pete showed me how to lift the cover of the cesspit near the house. It was slightly blocked so he showed me how to poke the waste in order to free the flow. It was an interesting process for a cook.

After being shown the cesspit I realised that the lamps were the last mystery. The Maenllwyd has no electricity and we rely on paraffin lamps, along with candles and torches. The lamps are hung by their handles from hooks around the beams and ceilings of the house. The air is pressurised by a hand-pump. There are mantles, wicks, and bits. I get dizzy, they confuse me, and I often feel lost just looking at them.

I have been shown how to use them many times, but I am reluctant to engage with them. I don't know what it is about them; they feel too masculine, rigid and mechanical. I depend on them but I choose not to connect with them. Yet I love their hissing and a vigorous, freshly-lit lamp as the day starts to turn makes me happy.

During this retreat I made an effort to connect with the lamps. I realised my feelings were changing when the red lamp, the most beautiful one, passed away; it would be scrapped for parts. Would she hiss again in another shape, would there be an essence of red in an army lamp?

I was eager to get ahead of myself, so that I could spend more time in the Chan Hall. I made a fragrant dhal using tiny cardamom seeds as a starting point, adding lots of fresh ginger, turmeric and a cinnamon stick. I also made barley miso rolls, by adding a couple of spoonfuls of miso to the bread dough, before the second kneading.

I made brownies and sprinkled them with different colour cornflowers I had dried in the summer. The dark brown richness of the brownies contrasted beautifully with the summer colours of the cornflowers. I started a curry base.

I was eager to get things prepared ahead of time because I wanted to join in the dance meditation. I danced with my eyes closed: a woman's dance. In the past I had danced with the little girl in me, embracing her, attempting to help her mend her heart. Now I felt that the little girl had grown up; she no longer believed herself ugly, fat or poor, or that she did not belong. As I danced, I was that girl full of potential, and the woman who was ready to open up to the world. A woman who was ready to live and to love. The wounds had healed, I had learned to make friends with my ghosts; I had asked them to tell me what they needed. This had been enough to appease them. I had nourished them and they had quietened down to rest.

As I danced with myself, it felt like an awakening. This was my life, and I would seize it.

I had learned to ask. This had been my biggest lesson. For so many years I resisted asking for help. I had been closed up, as if in an iron chest. Asking implies an opening, an acceptance of the vulnerability that makes us more connected to ourselves. By asking, I opened a channel which allowed the light in, and with light came space.

That night I had a dream. Once on a trip to Fes, in Morocco, my friend Ceci and I had visited a tiny antiques stall. We were fascinated by the beautiful objects exhibited behind locked glass, and the antiques dealer invited us to visit the back of the shop. We went through a low door, and as we lifted our heads we entered a different world, a magnificent *riad*, like the Aladdin's cave I had imagined as a child. There were rooms and rooms of the most delightful collection of objects I had ever seen: ancient Toureg rugs, woodcarvings, embroideries and jewelry. The place in my dream had a similar shop front: a small unimpressive room filled with beautiful clutter. The antiquarian, who was a different man from the one in Fes, looked Ceci in the eyes, and said, "You are a jeweller."

He held out his closed, cupped hands towards her, as if cradling something precious. He opened his hands to reveal a blue jewel, and said, "This jewel is for you, this is all the treasure you need to be happy."

Ceci took the jewel and thanked him, then he turned around to look at me, with eyes like a young doe. He told me, "Flo, you are a nomad. For you I also have something special."

He went into an adjacent little room and brought out a metal object, an oracle. He placed it on the wooden counter and unlocked the top. It opened up like a spinning metal top, a shiny carousel, and light, a white dense smoke, began to emanate from the object. I saw glimpses of my life: special occasions; ordinary routines; faces of loved ones, alive and dead. He invited me to look at how wonderful my life had been, and I did. I was able to see it all. I liked it, even the parts I had never liked before. He also showed me the future, a cloudy mass which was slightly further away from where I stood. He insisted that I should open up to my life and seize it.

A few weeks after I had the dream, Ceci called to tell me she was pregnant.

The wind was so strong it kept setting off the alarms of the cars in the yard, cars with nowhere to go yet. The wind carried rain from deep Atlantic storms, arriving in the mountain with the smell of the sea. I watched the sheep as they tasted the salt through their woolly skins.

I returned to my question: "Tell me who you are."

As I riddled the Rayburn and fed it coal, I was the child of Scottish coal miners who walked the Ayrshire winters barefoot as children.

As I buried my face in my hands as I sat down to lunch I smelt yeast and flour and dough; I was the child of French bakers who understood the secret ingredient in breadmaking.

As words trickled out of me through my pen, I was the child of writers.

As I walked up the hill, wind blowing my hair around in spirals, my face wet and each pore and cell, each atom, alive, I was the child of woman, fostered by nature.

Simon, who had succeeded John as Teacher of the WCF, was also taking part on this retreat. On the first night, he told me that he heard owls, and I longed to see one.

"Have you seen the owl?" I asked.

"No, why, do you want to see it?"

"No, I want to be it."

To me, owls have always symbolised knowledge and freedom, the wisdom that I seek.

Many years ago, I held a baby owl at a country fair. I remember gazing into its staring orange eyes, wanting to hold the moment forever. I felt a connection beyond language, an otherness in the ordinary.

The sycamores resembled giant, black spiders' webs, intricate against the backdrop of the sky. There were mossy patches everywhere, sprouting into tiny forests: moss giving birth to green goblins.

I went for an interview. I was so happy, but what would happen if I fell off the 100 foot pole of happiness that I felt I was on? Eddy reassured me that the fall wouldn't be too bad.

My mind kept dropping and all that was left for me to be was my heart. I felt like a fearless queen, connected with everything and nothing. This was a new experience, lived at a different pace. I was inhabiting a space that was more to do with my torso than with my head, my usual ruler.

Owl woman, take flight. Dance. I was ready to make the necessary changes, to shift the stagnant, cross-generational karma for the sake of my kids and for the sake of the women in my family who chose safe instead of wild. That evening I danced with my daughter, my mother, my sisters, my grandmothers and their mothers. It felt like I was beginning again.

"Tell me who you are?"

"I am...home."

The paraffin lamps were working a treat. Pete told me to drop the fear and start connecting with them. He told me to pump them twenty times each time I left the kitchen, and they kept alight for me.

The lamps with their leaky wonder evoked a memory of the stoves of my childhood winters. I remembered pulling clothes over my head as I stood by them and the drafts and shivers as they were lit, their brawny tang of heat. I remembered the paraffin barrel on stilts in the garden, the tap always shut tight. I used to climb astride it when nobody was watching, wriggle on the rusty metal and kick it, saying "*arre, arre, caballo*", as I rode my imaginary suburban horse.

One of the participants came to the back kitchen to talk to me.

"I am very upset about the hungry ghosts."

"Why?"

"Can't we feed them properly?"

"We do," I said, "They have narrow throats which only crumbs can go through. Their hunger and thirst and fear cannot be appeased by the crumbs, but it is the heart that you put in the offering which helps them."

"But we should give them a proper meal," she said, almost with tears in her eyes.

I felt like telling her that she was feeding them properly, because she was offering them her love, but I remained silent. She needed to work this one out for herself.

An Apollinaire poem kept popping into my mind:

> Come to the edge.
> We might fall.
> Come to the edge
> It's too high!
> Come to the edge!
> And they came.
> And he pushed,
> And they flew.

That night I danced again. This time, I was the owl ready to take flight, feet on the ground, my red toenails hinting at their ancestral past. I let go of the room and felt my legs, my waist, my shoulders. Sensing my joy, I stretched out and flew. I called on the owl in me to be daring, not to fear. I would be the one pushing myself off the edge.

I thought of the kitchen and stopped moving, while everyone else was still dancing. I remembered all I had to do: arrange the aubergines on platters; toast sunflower seeds and taste the saffron yogurt dressing for seasoning. I needed to warm the tagine with care: the wok was filled to capacity and the food at the bottom could easily burn. It would be impossible to stir without making the sweet potatoes disintegrate. All of the sudden I realised I was no longer present in the dance, so I gently left the barn. As I shut the door behind me, I was startled by a cacophony of owl sounds: hooting and screeching. I stood in the yard by the gate with a grinning heart. The owls were calling each other and I was encircled by their calls. I moved to the kitchen where their cries accompanied me as I carried food into the refectory. I could still hear them as we ate supper, even above the hissing of the paraffin lamp above the table.

After supper, I showed the "hungry ghosts" retreatant how to offer the bowl of water and scraps. She looked at me blankly and then at the bowl, as if not convinced. She later described what happened after I left:

"I had a beautiful experience making the offering, which I owe to you. After the initial surprise/disappointment of the unceremonious gate and field beyond where you left me, I looked down into the bowl. The fat in the food had picked up shades of red and gold. I swished it about and it made an emulsion. In the dark, in the light of my head torch, it was as if one hundred billion gems were reflecting back at me. It was spectacularly beautiful. So I offered countless jewels: tiny ones, small enough and enough in number. This experience made me realise that what I can do for others has to come from the heart."

I left the volunteers drying up, wrapped my long, woolly cardigan and several scarves around me and lay down on the bench in the back garden. I closed my eyes and I was with the owls; it felt like the noise was coming from a different realm yet it was there, coming from the trees, bouncing from sycamore to cypress, from maple to pine to cherry tree. I could still hear them when I went back to John's room and took up my pen to write. I could still hear them when, after the night sit, I returned to the bedroom. They hooted all night and into the dawn. The owl called from the mountaintop: "Come to the edge, come, fly."

Chapter Nineteen

Fly

July at the Maenllwyd. The weather was warm. The water level of the stream was very low, so the milk was going off very quickly; even the small dam we had built was not holding enough water in the flowing semi-pond to keep the bottles chilled. I wrapped the crates in soaked hessian sheets to help keep them cool, but I knew I would have to venture out to the shops at some point. In the kitchen, fresh herbs were rotting and vegetables were growing soft. The bread was going mouldy and swarms of flies danced around the shelves above the sink. They were distracting me, buzzing about me, hovering around the treacle and jams. I had to restrain myself from swatting them with a tea towel; after all, I had taken a vow not to kill.

Shoo Fly.

Shoo.

I became more and more aggravated by them. There were dozens of them: an invasion. I tried to get them out of the kitchen by waving my linen apron around. I was a cook possessed by my need to protect the food I offered.

After the rest period in the early afternoon, I sat by Tara's statue, under the trio of sycamores. The sycamores looked like beardy, old men with their bark wisdom and hollow trunks, keeping a watch on me. I had brought a parsley plant with me, as I needed some to flavour the evening meal. I have learned not to chop herbs but rather tear them, gently, and the difference in taste is remarkable. So I began my task, lost in the moment, looking at the plant with its green rosettes. I observed each line on each tiny leaf, split it slowly, carefully, lovingly and placed the small fragments into a metal bowl. I was enjoying the warmth, the company of the trees and the intensity of green against the glimmering silver of the bowl. Suddenly a fat house fly landed on my knee. I felt its tickly weightless body on mine. I saw her large eyes; they resembled the centre of the sunflower I had brought for the altar in the refectory. Her front legs rubbed her face. Her antennae moved as she gently flicked her wings. I observed her – microscopically.

"What do you want, Fly? Have you come to tell me something?"

I was taken by the insect's presence, by her beauty. It was a moment of feeling at one with the universe: a Fly moment. I couldn't take my eyes of her and I watched as she sank her minuscule legs into the cotton fibres of my trousers. Was she looking at me? I felt warmth arising from my heart. A love for the fly.

A guilty thought arose: I have killed so many. Insecticide, fly traps, wet tea towels: you name it, I have done it. Not because I liked doing it, but it was what you did to keep food safe, to preserve cleanliness. In hot places, flies are pests that threaten your food with their disease-carrying shit.

In La Granja, as children, during the long, boring siestas, we developed an obsession with trying to catch flies.

Sometimes it would take hours before we could, in a snap, hold a fly in our hand. We would wait for a fly to land near us, and then we would grab it, snap it, trying to be quicker than the fly. Most of our attempts failed. Once we caught one, we would play "Make a Fly a Pet". This game involved tying a long strand of hair from the head of one of the girls around the fly's body to hold it captive. The fly became like a miniature balloon with wings, desperate to take flight. It felt like a hero moment: "Look at what I got, a Fly Pet." We would keep it for a while, amuse ourselves as it struggled, held by an almost invisible thread. Then we would finally let it go, the poor exhausted fly.

Who was the first person who told me to kill a fly? Growing up, killing flies was almost a summer ritual. We cleaned the kitchen after every meal, covered everything and sprayed insecticide around the room. At least once a week we washed the brick floors of the patio with a few drops of creosote to make flies go away. My grandmother was usually armed with a flyswatter, exterminating the last few flies before she shut the door on the kitchen.

The thought of taking the life of such a beautiful insect filled me with sadness. A familiar desolation descended on me, one I often feel when I think how uncaring we are with the life around us. Then I felt grateful for the moment, for the teaching that this fly was offering me.

A few minutes later, Fly went about her business and I got back to the parsley.

Later on that day, after serving afternoon tea and cake in the garden, I joined the group for the chanting session in the Chan Hall. We were chanting a mantra in English. It was sung almost as a hymn, which I found difficult to engage with: the words were beautiful but there were too many of them and it felt a bit churchy to me. The room was warm as we had to keep the stove lit for hot water, so the windows were open. The hot air made the space feel as if it was seething, as if each individual was multiplying just like the flies in the kitchen.

Flies were buzzing about. Two or three kept landing on my arm and got between my fingers, crawling around inside my mudra (the position in which we hold our hands in meditation). To start with, I felt aggravated by the flies invading my palms and fingers. Then I remembered my Fly and began to feel the little flies as they touched my skin. My heart opened, I dropped the annoyance. Distracted by the tickling sensation they created, I snapped both my hands shut, like I did when I was a young girl. In each hand I was holding a Fly.

Rather than the feeling of prowess I used to feel as a child, I felt humbled and touched by the flies in my hands, by the beauty of the moment, by the connection to my previous encounter with the Fly under the sycamores. I could feel the tears filling my eyes. I felt like tapping the Guestmaster with my elbow to show her but I kept the moment to myself and, for a second, I observed the room. Everyone was lost in their chanting and breathing. The flies were struggling and my hands remained shut. I could feel them buzzing against my palms. I held them there for a while, just to feel them. Then I opened my hands and, gazing at their freedom, smiled.

Essential Elements of the Zen Kitchen

Whenever I create a meal for a retreat, I attempt to bring into play the contrasts that give dishes a specific balance, hoping that in each bite people can savour the different flavours of each ingredient, as they come together in one harmonious plate of food.

Cutting vegetables and the handling of ingredients requires attention, and in the Zen kitchen it is elevated to an art form. Simple tasks like chopping or washing feel worthwhile and satisfying.

I love cooking on an open flame. Cooking with fire is like cooking with sunshine and I have never been able to bond with electric rings or ceramic hobs. In my opinion, fire enlivens food.

Whenever I source food I try to get the best quality ingredients. If you work with good ingredients, the food will sing as you cook it; you will need to intervene much less. I prefer to use organic eggs, flours, grains, root vegetables and oranges. Whenever I mention orange zest in a recipe, I would only use organic. I would also recommend brushing the skin of the orange before zesting it.

We are lucky to have a wonderful pantry in the Maenllwyd in which we store the basics. Over the years I have found that there are certain things that I tend to use all the time.

Miso paste

Miso is a fermented soybean paste. It is a major ingredient in Japanese cooking, used in soups, stocks and dressings. I like to add it to the dough when I make bread and muffins.

Tamari sauce

Tamari is the original soy sauce. It is made by collecting the liquid which drains from miso as it ages. In Japan, tamari soy sauce is mainly produced in the Chubu region, where it is also known as miso-damari. In the UK you can buy it in wholefood shops and in some supermarkets. Most wholefood co-operatives stock big bottles of tamari, and I suggest you order one. I guarantee that you will begin to fall in love with the quality it adds to food and will think twice before you use ordinary soy sauce instead.

Umeboshi plums

Umeboshi pickled plums are a sweet and sour fruit product popular in Asian cultures and now available in most wholefood shops. The ume plums are pickled and dried in the open air. Then they are packed in sea salt and sisho leaves, pressed and aged for at least six months. They offer a variety of health benefits. You can use them whole, or in a paste; you can also find them in liquid form. I like them in miso soup, or as an addition to other soup bases – I add them as I fry the onions.

Mirin

Mirin is a sweet sake or rice wine that has the texture of a clear, light syrup. It is normally used in Japanese cooking and I like to experiment with it. It gives a mild sweetness to sauces and it is useful when you are trying to avoid using sugar to make food taste less acidic.

A complete spice rack

I buy my spices by the weight and often develop dishes just because I am eager to use a certain spice. I keep them in jars and tins, and love searching for good spice blends.

Good quality oils, always cold-pressed and extra virgin

I cook with extra virgin olive oil or cold-pressed sunflower oil wherever I can, but I sometimes use ordinary, good quality sunflower oil for cakes and curries.

Pomegranate molasses

Pomegranate molasses have a very distinct, smoky-sweet flavour and I am still finding different ways of using this ingredient. I talk about it in more detail in the chapter on Pomegranates. It isn't always easy to find, nor is it cheap, but it is worth it. You can find it online at **http://webstore.otto-lenghi.co.uk/collections/pantry**

Good quality balsamic vinegar

Recently, York has been invaded by delis that sell excellent quality balsamics stored in big barrel bottles, from which I decant the vinegars into my own bottles. Amongst my favourites are fig and pomegranate. A good balsamic can really enhance a dish, almost taking it to a different dimension.

Sea salt flakes

I use Maldon, but other sea salt brands are good too.

Herbs

I very rarely use dried herbs. I buy them fresh in bunches and in pots and I love the way they enliven a plate of food.

Some words on preparing vegetables

Vegetables need to be stored and kept fresh until you are about to cook them. Firstly, wash them carefully. Whether you are tenderly rinsing leaves or scrubbing mucky carrots, this is your first opportunity to begin connecting with them, as you start to think about how you are going to cut and prepare them. A vegetable that comes into contact with water often revives slightly and if you look carefully you might be able to "see" it in all its splendour.

The way we cut vegetables is also very important. The way they are sliced provides a keynote to how a dish will eventually look.

Make sure you have a sharp knife, a clean board and a bowl in which to put your vegetables. Have you decided what role your vegetable will play in the dish? Is it the star, or is it there as a base note flavour? Centre yourself in front of the board, remembering that your energy is going into the chopping, to enhance the vegetable. Sizes should be uniform to avoid unevenly cooked vegetables.

Food preparation can be a meditative practice; your awareness and attention should be on the food you are preparing, on the people you are preparing it for. Put your heart into it.

On my first retreat I was taught how to chop onions using macrobiotic principles, by following the onion's natural line and giving it the thickness that you need for the meal. When I started chopping onions like this at home I noticed that the flavour was different, that the onions kept a beautiful shape. They cooked better too. I really enjoy giving shape to vegetables for my dishes, or instructing assistants on retreats. I have developed different ways of cutting and have never since then used a food processor to chop a vegetable.

Vegetables should always be the stars of vegetarian dishes, so it is important to really allow them to shine in all their glory. Here are some different methods I use to help them do so.

Searing

Searing, or sealing, is my preferred method, as it allows vegetables to keep their crunch. In a heavy metal pan or a wok, with a tiny bit of oil, on a high heat, sauté the vegetables so that the contours are sealed and golden, but the inside remains firm. Do not let the vegetables lose their colour by cooking them too much.

Charring, or broiling

I grew up eating broiled or charred vegetables. For our meat-oriented barbecues in Argentina we used to place summer vegetables in the wood embers and burn the skin completely, then gently peel it off to reveal a smoky, fleshy vegetable: delicious. You can do the same under a hot grill or directly on a gas flame. Sweet peppers, aubergines and onions work a treat.

Roasting

Roast vegetables (or fruit) with extra virgin olive oil, sea salt, herbs and garlic. You name it, it can go in a roasting tin: potatoes, onions, squashes, courgettes, beetroot, tomatoes, fennel, endive, carrots, parsnips, apples, pears, sweet potatoes, peppers, celery, to name but a few. I like to heat up the oil first and toss the vegetables with herbs and seasoning.

Water frying

This is my preferred method for greens. Heat a little water in a wok, add your vegetables and a pinch of salt, give them a stir and cover. This is a quick method, so presence and speed are paramount. You don't want to overcook your chard or kale. You are steaming and boiling with the speed of a stir-fry.

Deep frying

This is not something I normally do, but I cannot resist a tempura of summer vegetables, or a plate of home-made chips, once in a while. The secret of deep frying is very hot oil and a good pan with a heavy base.

Steaming

Steaming helps preserve nutrients, enzymes and flavour. I don't have a steamer and it is possible to steam vegetables without one. Fill a saucepan with about an inch of water, add salt, and bring to a boil. Add the vegetables, turn to a simmer and cover. Be aware that different vegetables steam at different rates.

Blanching

I learned to blanch vegetables with my sister-in-law Jane in New York, as I helped her prepare endless baskets of crudités for cocktail parties. Blanching is easy and a wonderful way to preserve the colour, flavour and texture of vegetables. Cooking them quickly helps to tenderise them whilst allowing them to retain their crunch. Bring a large pot of water to a boil and add salt to taste. Make sure that you have all your vegetables prepared and ready. Get the cooling station ready while the water boils. Fill a bowl or a clean sink with cold water and ice. Only add small amounts of vegetables at a time to the boiling water, to make sure that the water does not come off the boil. Boil the vegetables for only a couple of minutes and remove them with tongs or a slotted spoon. Plunge them immediately in the iced cold water, then drain and rest them before serving.

Braising

Braising is a good way to cook vegetables that can be stringy or a bit tough, such as carrots, celery or parsnips. Ideally you should braise them with a pulse, so that they are not the star of the show. First seal the vegetables then cover them with liquid and cook in a casserole dish in the oven or on a very low flame.

Zen kitchen basic vegetable stock

There is nothing more comforting than a bowl of home-made soup, and nothing more predictable than a mass-produced stock cube: a gungey lump of salt and who knows what else. Even Marigold stock is too salty and thickens the soup too much. I like my broths to be clear and light so I find this irritating. I work on the seasoning once the soup is nearly ready; my favourite seasoning is tamari sauce.

This is why we make our own stock on retreats and why I make it at home too, as a base for a risotto, for a soup or for a pot pie. Here is a rough guide to a vegetable stock. It is appropriate for all the recipes in the book. Don't be shy with fresh herbs or with salt. Salt helps the flavour from the vegetables to seep into the broth). These are just guidelines, but remember that if the stock is too strong it might alter the flavour of your soup later on. Keep it simple, as the beauty of the stock is in its frugal taste. You will have space to tweak your soups with seasoning at a later stage.

You can vary what you put into the stock according to the soup you are planning to make. I like to add some kombu (seaweed) if I am going to make a miso soup; afterwards I slice it finely and add it to the soup. For dahl, I put in some fresh ginger and fresh coriander. Remember to use the tops and tails of your vegetables and the mushroom stalks. Be thrifty and inventive.

1 large onion (peeled as the skin can sometimes be too strong and bitter)
1 leek, trimmed and washed
A few celery stalks
2 or 3 carrots
1 potato, chopped, with the skin still on
A bunch of parsley
3 bay leaves
½ tsp salt
A few whole black peppercorns

Put all the ingredients into a pot of cold water. Leaving the lid off, simmer for approximately an hour. Drain directly into the soup, or into a container, to use later.

Vinaigrettes

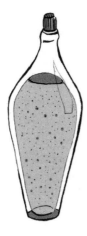

Vinaigrettes offer the perfect opportunity to become creative and to experiment with ingredients. Get a sense of what might go with your type of salad. Be adventurous; tweak. Adding condiments and spices to vinaigrettes takes them into a different dimension. You might try adding tahini, pomegranate molasses, toasted spices, orange or lemon zest, or chopped fresh herbs. Choose according to the season or to the type of oil you are using. Buy something you have never cooked with before and taste it: what do you think it would like to be mixed with? Here are some guiding recipes.

Classic vinaigrette

125 ml extra virgin olive oil
30 ml good quality balsamic vinegar
Sea salt

Mix all the ingredients together in a measuring jug or a jar with a screw top. Shake spiritedly. Toss over your salad before serving.

Summer vinaigrette

125 ml cold-pressed sunflower oil
½ tsp Dijon mustard
½ tsp runny honey
1 garlic clove, crushed
Sea salt

It is important to whisk this dressing so I generally use a large glass measuring jug. Add each ingredient at a time and mix with a small whisk or with a fork. Be moderate with the salt, as it is better to add more salt later straight into the salad. Trickle the lovely ochre dressing directly onto your salad, or transfer it into a jar.

Fragrant vinaigrette

   5 tbsp extra virgin olive oil
   4 tbsp good balsamic vinegar or cider vinegar
   3 tbsp water
   2 tbsp wholegrain mustard
   3 tbsp lemon juice
   2 tbsp chopped lovage or basil or chives
   A dash of tamari sauce

Follow the same instructions as for the summer vinaigrette.

My favourite Japanese vinaigrette

   2 tbsp cold-pressed toasted sesame oil
   ½ tbsp mirin
   2 tbsp brown sugar
   1½ tbsp tamari sauce
   75 g black sesame seeds

This dressing is perfect for greens, like kale or spring greens, served warm. It also works fabulously with blanched asparagus or green beans.

First toast the sesame seeds in a frying pan on a low heat until they begin to pop. Keep an eye on them so that they do not burn. Transfer the seeds into a pestle and mortar and crush them together with the sugar, the tamari, the oil and the mirin until you have a paste. Don't expect it to be smooth; the texture given by the seeds will complement the softness of the vegetables.

Miso vinaigrette

2 tbsp barley miso
1 tsp Dijon mustard
1 tbsp water
2 tbsp fresh lemon juice
125 ml extra virgin olive oil
2 tbsp cold-pressed sesame oil
1 tsp finely grated fresh ginger
A good dash of tamari sauce
2 spring onions, finely chopped

In a bowl whisk together the miso and the mustard and slowly add the water and the lemon juice. Then drizzle the oil in gently while whisking (this helps create a good emulsion). Add the tamari and ginger and leave to rest. Before serving, whisk again and add the spring onions. You can keep this dressing for up to a week in the fridge.

Acknowledgements

I was on retreat at the Maenllwyd when a deep wish arose to write a book about my cooking experiences. I shared this wish during a communication exercise with Sarah Bird, and when it was her turn to speak, she talked about creating an ethical publishing company. Now both Vala and *Feeding Orchids to the Slugs* have come into existence: both owe a great deal to that retreat.

I am deeply indebted to Sarah, she has been an incredible editor and friend; her enthusiasm, patience, painstaking care and hard work are visible on every page of this book.

For seven years I have worked away from home to cook on retreats. I always miss my children, Ian and Sofia, when I am away and I will refrain from telling the sheep story as they find it utterly annoying, but I must thank them for accepting my need to do this job, and for being so understanding when I needed to lock myself away to write.

As I write, a quote from the *The Little Prince* by Antoine de Saint-Exupéry comes to me: "It is only with the heart that one can see rightly; what is essential is invisible to the eye." Only now can I begin to comprehend Saint-Exupéry's words, and one person has helped me in this process: Simon, my partner of the last twenty years. He and his "child's eye" have helped me open the natural world to my own eyes, to my heart, to appreciate the perfect beauty of everything around us, which we are usually too shut-down or distracted to notice. He has offered me precious gifts, by helping me move towards a better understanding of who and what I am, towards waking up to my life. He has been fully supportive, not only of my journeys as a Zen cook, but also during the writing of this book. His only advice: put your heart into it.

Finding the Maenllwyd and The Western Chan Fellowship has been like finding my tribe. I bow to the late John Crook and to Simon Child, Jake Lyne, Hilary Richards, Ken Jones, Fiona Nuttall, Sophie Temple-Muir and Eddy Street. Their teachings and extensive support in interviews have helped shape the path I have been walking. I bow too to the long lineage of Maenllwyd cooks, and I will feel forever grateful to Miche Fabre-Lewin and Pamela Butler who inspired and trained me in the early days. I also thank Pete Lowry and Douglas Orton, for giving me encouragement every time I felt that I needed it, but did not dare to ask.

I offer deep thanks to all of the fellow retreatants with whom a great intimacy and rapport has developed through this silent practice.

My friends in Argentina always talk with nostalgia about my parents' house. They particularly remember the kitchen and the food my mum prepared. My parents gave me an enormous lesson in generosity. Even when there was little money there was always enough food to feed our friends and whoever turned up unannounced. My parents' philosophy was to cook and offer food to people with love, which they still practice effortlessly.

I thank my sisters Magdalena and Julieta, and Pablo, my brother, for the hours and hours of play and adventures; also for being the best siesta companions and enthusiastic supporters of my cooking.

I married into a family of wonderful cooks. Although their influence is present in each step of my cooking practice, their part in this story deserves its own book. Jane McQueen-Mason, my sister in law, runs a catering company in New York City and I loved working for her when I lived in the US. She made me the foodie I am today, introduced me to some unforgettable dishes, gave me cookbooks and shared her most secret recipes with me. I hope she writes her own book one day. Lucy McQueen-Mason, my mother-in-law, was the best cook I ever met. She had magic hands and she put her heart into every meal she cooked. I have often cooked with Lucy in mind on retreats, and lit candles in her memory, hoping that her wonderful skill with flavours could slip into my food. I owe Lucy my soup-making skills and I miss eating her field mushroom soup on late summer days on the Isle of Wight.

To Alec Lawless, who I met on one of my first retreats. He showed me that taste and smell have ruled the world since ancient times. You are missed.

To Julia Wheater, who has been the source of many great cookbooks, read the first words I wrote for this book and helped me type out the recipes.

To Hannah Davies: writing is a solitary process and sometimes it helps to share with someone else who is also writing. Her loving, critical approach and encouragement have been there to support me when I needed it most.

I met Michaela Meadow when she was a shy little girl who made and sold fairies at the Steiner School fair. I was lucky enough to watch her blossom as she moved to Falmouth to study illustration. The artistic activities of Michaela and her friends have been a constant source of inspiration for my own experimentation on retreats. Michaela's artwork has always resonated with my inner experience, and I was delighted when she agreed to create the illustrations for this book. Her paintings are directly inspired by each chapter and I am delighted to be working with her.

To Ned Reiter for writing the foreword to this book.

Heartfelt thanks to the courageous friends who read the first draft of the manuscript and gave valuable feedback: Pat Simmons, Hilary Richards, Clive Richards, Sophie Temple-Muir, Titus Forbes-Adam, Hugo Hildyard , Hannah Davies and Simon McQueen-Mason. And to our valued proofreaders: Pat Simmons, Freyja Atkins and Denis Kennedy.

Many thanks to the recipe testing team from Vala, particularly to Linda Broadbent who went far beyond the call of duty and blogged enthusiastically about the dishes in her *Veg Box Monologues*.

The Maenllwyd and the surrounding landscape of the Welsh mountains were a pivotal place for me to heal and change. Never before have I encountered a space that moved me and spoke to me so intimately. The house harbours a warmth that nurtures the heart. I will be forever grateful to John Crook for sharing his magical place with us.

I was lucky to move to the UK just in time for the gourmet revolution. No other chef has inspired me more than Jamie Oliver. I love his instinctual approach to food, his passion for good ingredients, and his mish-mash of delights. I learned so much just by watching him on television, and every single recipe of his that we tried became a favourite. Above all, his tireless quest to better the diet of people around the world makes him, in my eyes, a true Bodhisattva.

The first time I stepped into Ottolenghi's restaurant in Islington, I thought, "This is Zen food!" The big plates of salads, composed of grains, vegetables, nuts, seeds and herbs, celebrated not only colour and taste, but a fusion of cultures and methods in one dish. They were wonderful. When I first cooked from *Ottolenghi: The Cookbook* on retreat, it took me seven hours to prepare a feast for fourteen. Every mouthful was worth it, people moaned with delight in the silence of the refectory, and everyone wanted to know where I had got the ideas from. Some of Ottolenghi's dishes have somehow become my own.

I would like to thank Cathy Pelly who drowned when she was sixteen and whose memorial stone plays such an important role in my retreats on Bala Brook, and in the chapter "Dancing with Death".

And finally to the antiquarian *brujito* in my dream, who gave Ceci the jewel that we will cherish and showed me how wonderful my life has been, is and how magical it could be.

Index of Recipes

About Vala

Vala is an adventure
in community supported publishing.

We are a co-operative
bringing books to the world that explore and celebrate
the human spirit with brave and authentic
ways of thinking and being.

Books that seek to help us find our own meanings
that may lead us in new and *unexpected* directions.

Vala's co-operative members
- suggest authors
- design
- write
- support the writing process
- get together for book-making evenings
- promote and sell Vala books through their own networks.

Members come together to celebrate and launch each
new publication. Together we decide what happens to any
profit that we make.

Vala exists to bring us all into fuller relationship with our
world, ourselves, and each other.

To find out more visit us at *www.valapublishers.coop*

An Invitation

We hope that you have enjoyed reading *Feeding Orchids to the Slugs*.
We would welcome your comments and reviews at:

www.valapublishers.coop/feedingorchidstotheslugs
or at **www.facebook.com/feedingorchidstotheslugs**

where you can also see Florencia's photos of the locations and
recipes mentioned in the book.